A
HISTORY
of the
MID-SOUTH FAIR

A
HISTORY
of the
MID-SOUTH FAIR

EMILY YELLIN

GUILD BINDERY PRESS, INC.
MEMPHIS, TENNESSEE

GUILD BINDERY PRESS

Staff for: A History of the Mid-South Fair

Editor and Publisher: Randall Bedwell
Managing Editor: Robbin Brent
Executive Editor: David Yawn
Consulting Editors: Trent Booker and Michael Finger
Creative Director: Pat Patterson, Patterson Design Works
Cover and Layout Design: Greg Hastings

PUBLISHED IN MEMPHIS, TENNESSEE
by GUILD BINDERY PRESS, INC.

Library of Congress Cataloging-in-Publication Data

CIP
94-76776

Yellin, Emily

     A History of the Mid-South Fair / Emily Yellin
     p. cm.

ISBN 1-55793-046-5
Non-Fiction

Printed in the United States of America

1 2 3 4 5 6 7 8 9 10
First Edition

TABLE OF CONTENTS

ACKNOWLEDGEMENTS

INTRODUCTION

A C K N O W L E D G E M E N T S

The author wishes to thank the following people for their assistance and support during the research and writing of this book:

Mid-South Fair Board Presidents, Bobby Bowers 1992-1993, Bob Jamison 1994-1995 and Bill Todd 1996-1997

The Mid-South Fair Historical Committee: Edward F. Williams III, Chair; Hal Lewis; Robert L. Nichols

Jim Johnson, Patricia LaPointe and the entire staff of the Memphis Room and the History Department of the Memphis/Shelby County Public Library

Ed Frank and the entire staff of the Mississippi Valley Collection at the University of Memphis Library

Executive Editor David Yawn

Editorial Assistants Michelle Robinson and John Hershberger

With special personal thanks to:
Robert Dye, Jr., Michael Finger, Alistar Halloran, Daphne Hewett, Brenda Boudreaux, The Girls Institute and The Boys Auxiliary, Maria Miller, Merry Mariano, Jina Cohen, Aleece Hiller, John Beifuss, Kathy Steuer, Junius Harris, Neil Kramer, Darsey Mitchell, Karen Jozefowicz, Valerie Gutwirth, Lisa Zingale, Reneé Brotherton

and most especially David and Carol Lynn Yellin.

ℐn a book with so many photographs, the process of researching and gathering them all is complex. So it is essential to thank again the following people who patiently and generously cooperated in the complicated process of getting the many photos you see here from their various collections into this book.

Fair Presidents Bobby Bowers, Bob Jamison and Bill Todd, the fair Board of Directors and the entire staff of the Mid-South Fair for access to their offices, scrapbooks and photo files throughout this project.

Jim Johnson, Patricia LaPointe and the entire staff of the Memphis and Shelby County Room and the History Department of the Memphis/Shelby County Public Library and Information Center were nothing short of saintly in their dedication and efficiency. They have an extensive treasure trove of early photos of the fair and the fairgrounds to which they generously gave us access.

Ed Frank and the entire staff of the Mississippi Valley Collection at the University of Memphis always went the extra mile in helping us pore over the photo files of the *Memphis Press-Scimitar* in their collection. Their help proved invaluable in piecing together the photos of later fair history. We are also grateful to the many Memphis Press-Scimitar newspaper photographers whose work appears here.

Robert Dye, Jr. kindly made available his entire collection of photographs of the Mid-South Fair. He and his father have been independently documenting the fair and other Memphis events and landmarks since the late 1940s. Their family tradition added a lot to our efforts at showing all aspects of the fair through the years and we are extremely grateful for their cooperation and assistance.

Donne Walden and Alistar Halloran also contributed their own photographs to our efforts, and deserve our thanks.

And finally, a special thanks to David Yawn for invaluable help in selecting the photos to use, and to Michelle Robinson and John Hershberger for their tireless assistance in collecting and captioning the photos.

The Mid-South Fair touches more people in the Mid-South area than any other thing we do in Memphis. We have young and old, black and white, rich and poor, urban and rural. All segments of the community in this part of America are touched by the Fair, from the farms in Arkansas, Mississippi and Tennessee to the inner city of Memphis. There is something for everybody.

That's why I'm here. I've been involved with the Fair operation for 16 years, and I grew up coming to the Fair every year. It was always a big thing to me, and I think I'm more excited about it now than I was then.

To be a part of the Mid-South Fair is a very satisfying thing. It is a great family operation. We have a staff of about 30 and just hundreds of volunteers who love the Fair the same way I do.

Everyone involved is dedicated to making the Fair better every year. I would challenge anybody to point out anything that Memphis does better than presenting the Mid-South Fair. It is truly an honor to serve as President.

Bill Todd
President, Mid-South Fair

The full history of the Mid-South Fair is a story that is significant and long overdue. Growing up in Memphis, I got acquainted with the Fair as a child. As far back as I can remember, coming to the Mid-South Fair was a great tradtition and a great experience.

My official involvement with the Fair began as I worked with various committees of the Fair. Later, I became a certificate holder and board member. When Olin Morris completed his term as president, he tabbed me to enter the traditional 10-year process toward becoming president myself.

In recent years, we have achieved a bigger and better Fair, with increased attendance and revenues. We've been able to turn Libertyland around and make it profitable. We improved our midway, with a much improved show, better customer service, quality machinery, a strong labor force and a first-class presentation.

All that is the result of the cooperation of a lot of people, a real team effort. The officers are like a cork in the ocean, compared to the hundreds of volunteers who really make all this happen. They are cemented together and coordinated by General Manager Milton Rodgers and his staff. I cannot say enough good about them. It's genuinely been a great pleasure to be associated with them over the years. Without all these people, the Fair could not be a reality.

The strength of the Fair comes from the fact that it is a window into our community. It reflects who we are, from the commercial exhibits to the individuals who make quilts to the kids who raise livestock. People what to feel and touch and be a part of the Fair.

The Mid-South Fair has had its up and downs. But it has survived, grown and thrived because it is such a vital part of the community.

Bobby Bowers
Past President, Mid-South Fair

On behalf of the officers and the historical committee, I am very proud to be involved with this history book about our great Mid-South Fair. It contains some very special photos that bring back many memories for those of us who have been involved with the Fair. As a boy, I remember attending the Fair with my dad, who was a country boy at heart. We visited the cow, sheep and hog barns for hours. When we left the barns, we would head straight for the rides with a few stops at favorite food booths. One special event we saw was the Arena building rodeo. Boy, have we come a long way. Memories of those wonderful times certainly played a big part in my becoming a Fair volunteer.

Today, the Mid-South Fair/Libertyland, Inc., has grown to a $10-million operation and has employed thousands of young people. Though the Fair employs many people, we could not have a successful Fair without the dedication of our Fair Family of volunteers.

The Mid-South Fair is a 365-day-a-year job. We start planning for the next year while the current Fair is in progress. Our General Manager and the staff do a great job for us. They work with a different leader each two years when a new Board takes office, but when the gates open and the people start pouring in, it makes all of the hard work worthwhile.

I would like to thank everyone who has made my Presidency so meaningful, including the officers, staff, my family and my wife, Lynne, who is my best friend. I also would like to thank two very special people, Past President Jim Campbell, who was instrumental in my becoming a Fair volunteer, and Past President Oscar Edmonds, who nominated me for Board Office.

The thing I enjoyed most during my term has been the opportunity to be a part of something that has prospered for 140 years from now, there will still be a great Mid-South Fair.

Bob Jamison
President, Mid-South Fair

INTRODUCTION

It's hard to find many Memphis traditions that have endured as long or been as resilient as the Mid-South Fair. For nearly a century and a half, the fair has survived wars, epidemics, economic depressions, fires and social revolutions. And through all that, it still has managed to maintain its reputation for youthful fun, fascination, excitement and amusement. In fact, in learning about the history of the Mid-South Fair, one might even be excused for thinking there is some kind of magical fountain of youth somewhere which has helped give it the energy and timelessness that have kept it going in this region since its beginning in 1856.

But the Mid-South Fair has survived and thrived for much more simple and logical reasons. Most importantly, it has continued by remaining a relevant and important part of the region's society and economy. The fair is one of the few events that brings together all types of Mid-Southerners — young and old, urban and rural, black and white, farmers, business people, homemakers, entertainers and others. And the fair has woven its way into the political, social and economic development of the city and become a part of the fabric of Memphis.

Also, without being too highbrow and anthropological about it, there is still another important and more universal explanation for how the Mid-South Fair originally came into being, and why it has endured for so long. It is rooted in a deep historical tradition of our culture — a tradition of fairs that dates back to the beginning of Western civilization.

The word "fair" comes from the Latin word feria, meaning a holiday or feast day. But fairs were held before the Romans. Thousands of years ago, the first fairs of ancient times were started to carry on peaceful trade between different tribes. Tribesmen from far and wide would come together at certain spots to exchange goods. These tribes were often at war with each other, but they declared a truce at the "fair ground," which they regarded as a holy place. It was believed that the gods would punish anyone who fought or cheated there.

These early fairs were always linked with religious matters. The ancient Arabs, Egyptians and Irish all had such fairs. In ancient Greece fairs were held in conjunction with festivals honoring the gods. They were high-class events, and considered very important. In fact, the famous Olympic games were even held at one such fair. Fine goods were sold, not just cheap trinkets. A Greek fair-goer could find the finest glassware, cloth, spices, carpets and armor for sale. Trade at Greek fairs was controlled by the priests, who had the unlikely but important job of money changing, and could even lend money to trustworthy merchants. Because of the almost holy nature of these fairs, a crime at a fair was much more severely punished than it would have been if committed anywhere else.

The Romans had a special goddess of fairs and harvests. She was called Feronia, and festival-like Roman fairs centered around celebrating her. But the Romans also had fairs which were not a part of any religious ceremony and were designed solely for trade. The day these fairs were held became a holiday and country people would bring their produce to the grounds and exchange it for cloth and other manufactured articles. Special officials were chosen at all fairs to see that business was done in an orderly, peaceful and honest way. A whole set of business laws grew out of the rules that were made for these Roman fairs. And people who came to these fairs were protected from all harm; nobody could be arrested at a fair for a crime committed elsewhere.

When the Roman Empire declined and Christianity began to spread, fairs evolved further. They were held in honor of Christian saints instead of the old pagan gods. European fairs became centers for trade in the Middle Ages. And for the first time, amusement became part of the fairs in the later Middle Ages with acrobatics, tightrope dancing and fire eating.

An American twist on the fair tradition was the development of agricultural fairs, which became popular in the United States in the early 1800s. These fairs were less about trade than about showcasing products. Prizes were given for contest winners. In those early fairs the main prizes were for livestock, but other products garnered awards as well. Also, for the first time in the history of fairs, women took an active part in these early American agricultural events. They sent in their jellies, pickles, mincemeat and other homemade goods and received medals and prizes for the best. As the tradition grew, quilting bees, athletic contests and horse races became a part of American fairs as well.

At the same time these agricultural fairs were developing in rural areas, industrialization was taking place in the cities. So in urban areas, expositions, where industrial, commercial and scientific developments were featured, became popular. The largest of these was the 1851 Crystal Palace Exposition of the "Industry of All Nations" in London, organized by the London Society of Arts. More than six million visitors saw exhibits by 15,000 exhibitors. Among the principal exhibits were such inventions as the McCormick reaper and the Colt repeating pistol. Other expositions soon followed. The New York Crystal Palace Exposition of 1853 featured the first passenger elevator and demonstrations of the sewing machine.

Inevitably, some of the agricultural fairs and urban expositions met and melded, and evolved into regional events. Indeed, this is how the Mid-South Fair, which took the best of those early fair traditions and added a dash of local flavor, became the celebrated Memphis institution it is today.

From its beginnings as the Shelby County Fair in 1856, through its expansion into the Tri-State Fair in the 1910s and 1920s, and its further growth into the modern Mid-South Fair known today, the story of this annual fall gathering is an engrossing one. It is surprising, exciting and full of almost as many ups and downs as the fair's trademark Pippin roller coaster. But just like the Pippin, the Mid-South Fair has kept going, and has continued to capture the imaginations of successive generations of Memphians. Because of that appeal, the story of the Mid-South Fair offers a chronological window through which some of the heart and soul, and much of the growth and survival, of the city of Memphis and her surrounding areas can be seen and appreciated. Unfortunately, while there are no pictures to document the first 50 years of fairs in Memphis, the many photos that exist from then on provide echoes of those early fairs which inform us about the past. Although the spectacles, the animals, the people, and the food may have changed, the fun and the wonder that have kept the crowds coming back year after year are timeless, making the Mid-South Fair one of Memphis' most durable, fascinating and longest-running events.

CHAPTER
One

The First 50 Years of Fairs in Shelby County

1856-1906

1856-1860 PRE-CIVIL WAR YEARS

THE 1856 FAIR - MEMPHIS' FIRST

*I*n the mid-1850s the United States was 80 years old and Memphis, which had been a city for fewer than 40 years, was an emerging river port. Its location on the river and at the intersection of three rich agricultural states — Tennessee, Arkansas and Mississippi — put the city in a prime position to become an important distribution and merchandising center.

Agriculture and industrialization came together in Memphis. But during the time Memphis was emerging as a major regional city, frontier conditions prevailed, and there were not the kinds of transportation and communication links that would come later. Needless to say, there were no phones, no fax machines, no cars, no airplanes, no televisions. In fact, in the 1850s there weren't even electric light bulbs. So one of the main challenges of the time, in both the business and social realms, was to find ways to meet and communicate with others in the region. In response, the Shelby County Agricultural Society was formed in 1854 to promote the interests of not only local planters and farmers, but also of the merchants and businessmen of the community.

*I*n its second year of existence, the Society decided to stage a fair in the fall of 1856, under the leadership of Col. John Pope, a prominent planter in Shelby County and the president of the Society. Fairs were becoming popular events throughout the country, and were centered around showcasing goods and products. Merchandise was exhibited and displayed, and competitions were held. This was just what the Agricultural Society members felt Shelby County needed.

The stated aim of the first Shelby County Fair, as it was then called, was to exhibit and promote the area's finest products. Or, in the rather more elegant words of the sponsoring Agricultural Society, the event was organized for "farmers, merchants, tradespeople, gentlemen and gentle ladies to present their wares, products and handiwork for the evaluation of judges and the affirmation of their neighbors."

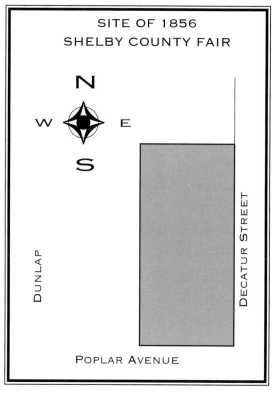

SITE OF 1856
SHELBY COUNTY FAIR

DUNLAP

DECATUR STREET

POPLAR AVENUE

sunny and mild both days, and fully half of Memphis' more than 12,000 residents came out. Of course, many popular elements of present-day fairs, such as the attractions of the Midway or Miss Mid-South Fair pageant, were not a part of the fair in 1856. But the 1856 Shelby County Fair included the beginnings of the idea that the fair should always exhibit the best in agricultural produce and the latest in machinery and inventions. The "best and the latest" is still the emphasis of present-day fair exhibits.

Some of the activities of the 1856 fair are still regular features almost a century and a half later at present-day Mid-South Fairs. For example, the first fair awarded cash prizes, or premiums, for the best of various exhibits and contests. There were prizes for best cake, cooked ham, butter, and preserved peaches and pears. And since cotton was omnipresent in the Memphis economy even then, prizes also were awarded for best cotton bale, cotton stalks and cotton samples, and best cotton mattress.

That first fair was held on October 22 and 23, 1856, in a temporary location described as a "serene grove" located "near Mr. Brinkley's place on State Line Road." In present-day Memphis, what was then called State Line Road is now called Poplar Avenue. The location of the 1856 fair has been pinpointed as a nine-acre plot of land just north of present-day Poplar Avenue and west of Decatur Street in the Pauline Circle area of Memphis. Dixie Homes now stands on this location, just a few blocks west of where Poplar Avenue crosses I-240. While today the area could hardly be called serene, in 1856, it was on the eastern outskirts of Memphis.

Although the first fair was hastily organized and lasted only two days, it was well-attended. The weather, always a factor in fair attendance, was

By the mid-1990s the total of premiums awarded at the Mid-South Fair had reached more than $260,000. The total of all the premiums awarded for the 1856 fair amounted to $350. Yet the first fair was profitable; the Agricultural Society ended up with a surplus of about $450 which it used to expand and to help finance the next year's fair.

As much as any that would come after it, that first Shelby County Fair reflected the richness and variety of the community's resources and quality of life. Samples of skill in embroidery, handkerchiefs, woolen hose and ottoman covers were exhibited.

Produce such as turnips, sweet potatoes, and tomatoes, as well as corn, millet, wheat and rye was abundant. Moreover, fair-goers saw livestock, including horses, ducks, cows and bulls, as well as the latest in agricultural implements and manufactured goods.

Since the first fairs took place before the Civil War, many of the farmers in the region still owned slaves. Interestingly, the slaves were not barred from taking part in the exhibits and competition. A newspaper of the era tells that a premium was awarded at the 1856 fair to "a negro of Rice Bond's for the best plowing collar." The premiums could be ten dollars or more in silver, or they could be copies of current agricultural journals such as the *Georgia Cultivator* or the *Tennessee Farmer and Mechanic*.

Not merely for exhibits and competitions, the first fair also served as a social event and an outlet for entertainment. Thus, two other features of the 1856 fair proved to be big attractions for many area residents. One was an equestrian performance judged by ladies. Twenty-seven men and their mounts competed for the prizes offered. More importantly perhaps, there was oratory, which proved to be a big draw at the time.

On opening day at the first fair, Colonel Henry J. Cannon of Fayette County delivered an address. He generally praised the fair and pointed out to his audience that they were attending the first exhibition of its kind to be held in Shelby County. He went on to say he hoped it would produce "goodly fruit" and be an example to other counties to "go and do likewise." Rice Bond was another featured orator at that first fair. His presentations were praised by the *Memphis Appeal* as "the most impres-

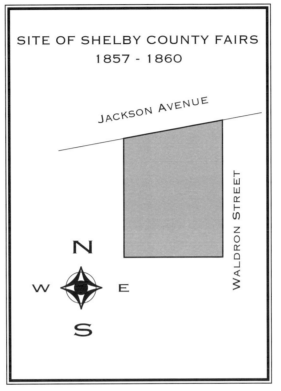

SITE OF SHELBY COUNTY FAIRS
1857 - 1860

JACKSON AVENUE

WALDRON STREET

N
W E
S

sive and eloquent agriculture addresses that it has been our pleasure to listen to."

The paper continued in the flowery style of the day to say, "Yesterday was indeed a gala day in Shelby County, and the pleasure derived by a large portion of our population who were so fortunate as to attend the Fair, and witness the agreeable scenes there presented, can never be eradicated as this, the first exhibition of the Agricultural and Mechanical articles, in an epoch in the history of Shelby County." That may have been a dramatic way of saying it, but the point made is true. The 1856 Shelby County Fair was an important event in the history of this region because it was the beginning of a tradition that was to grow and change with Memphis and become a meaningful event in the life of its residents.

1857 - 1860 FAIRS

For the next four years, until the Civil War, the Shelby County Fair was held at what was intended to be its permanent location. The Shelby County Agricultural Society signed a ten-year lease on an area located a few blocks north of where the 1856 fair was held. It was on about ten acres of land just west of the present intersection of I-240 and Jackson Avenue (which at the time was called Raleigh Road). That area was described back then as about a mile and a half north of Memphis.

Despite the success of the 1856 fair, not everyone was convinced of the value of a fair for the region. Public opinion can be made to order, however, and there is no doubt that the newspapers enthusiastically supported it. For example, the *Memphis Daily Bulletin* boosted the fair this way: "Our lands are rich, our climate delightful and our productions abundant. But to stimulate enterprise and diversified crops, there is no remedy like well-conducted fairs."

More frequently in these pre-Civil War years, speakers featured at the fairs were from outside of Shelby County. This fact points to the widening regional scope of the Shelby County Agricultural and Horticultural Fair, as it was called by then. In 1857 the ex-governor of Tennessee, James C. "Lean Jimmy" Jones spoke. And in 1858, Colonel J.J. Williams, secretary of the Mississippi Agricultural Bureau and editor of the *Planter and Mechanic* in Jackson was the main speaker.

For those who did not wish to travel to the 1858 fair by horse and buggy, the Memphis and Ohio Railroad provided transportation from the city depot to the fairgrounds for half fare — ten cents each way. And to attract visitors from farther-away places, the Memphis and Charleston Railroad offered excursion tickets to Memphis for the entire week of the fair.

By 1858 the fair ran for four days. The permanent fairgrounds now held an amphitheater and a Floral Hall where ladies' exhibits were displayed. One feature added to the fair in 1858 harked back to the medieval heritage of fairs. It was a "Grand Tournament" in which 22 "Knights" competed in riding and jousting events. The champion Knight was to be awarded a $50 pitcher and was entitled to name the Queen of Love and Beauty. The next two most successful Knights were to select the first and second Maids of Honor. But the Knights of Shelby County were obviously not very adept at this kind of tournament. Many of the riders were thrown from their horses, and the tournament was abruptly ended when one of the Knights was seriously injured in a fall. That marked the beginning and the end of the Grand Tournament at the Shelby County Fair.

However, in 1858 a more enduring tradition started — harness racing. This was the most popular form of horse racing in the United States in the 1800s. The horses pulled small two-wheeled vehicles which

were called sulkies (and were vaguely reminiscent of Roman chariots) around a track. In the Memphis papers it was described as a "trial of skill in buggy driving." There were five entries in that first contest. In the course of a race one of the sulkies was upset: The driver was thrown from his seat, and the horse was turned over on his back. After the crowd saw that neither the driver nor the horse was injured, they helped turn the vehicle right side up. The driver cracked his whip and "was off in a twinkling, amid the most vociferous shouting and huzzaing and waving of handkerchiefs." As he rounded the track in front of the ladies, "his buggy was covered by a shower of bouquets which came near causing another upset." Harness racing continued at the fair until the 1930s as the race track became an increasingly important part of Mid-South Fair history.

Visitors to the 1858 fair could also see the best and latest exhibits. On display were cooking ranges, stoves and three makes of sewing machines. According to the *Memphis Daily Appeal* of October 13, 1858, "a child's dress and a suit of boy's clothes, made upon one of Singer's Sewing Machines, by a lady who has had only four months' practice in its use, are among the most tasteful and elegant articles of the kind we ever saw." The reporter added, "The work executed by the Singer's Sewing Machine . . . is an object of general admiration." While the sewing machine exhibits amazed and enthralled many observers, there seemed to be differing reasons why. The paper's report explained, "The sewing machine is an object of interest to the ladies; the operator, to the gentlemen."

Also on display were "buggies, rockaways and other light pleasure vehicles of the latest design." A dentist exhibited "a set of artificial teeth and specimens of his work in dentistry" which were said to be "equal to anything of the kind to be found in the United States." There were also the usual produce, livestock, needlework, culinary and mechanical exhibits in 1858, as well as "a rich display in the Fine Arts, consisting of oil paintings, crayons, engravings and daguerreotypes."

And finally there was the food. Visitors could visit the food booths to eat everything from appetizers to "railroad stew," a complete meal. However, no alcohol was allowed. Article 12 of the Agricultural Society's by-laws said, "Spirituous liquors shall not be sold or drank [sic] upon the grounds of the Fair."

Despite all these attractions, by 1858 the fair was still not garnering the support from the community that it needed. Perhaps the event had lost some of its novelty. It seemed many people in Shelby County, and Memphis in particular, did not appreciate the advantages that grew out of fairs. The mixed reception the fair was getting was reflected in the way the *Memphis Daily Appeal* first commented on how improved exhibitions and contests of the fair had increased public interest, but went on to point out, "These are most gratifying evidence of a steady progress and improvement in agricultural and mechanical knowledge and skill, and we look forward to the time when we shall be able to give a practical refutation to the long prevalent idea, that Fairs cannot succeed in a planting country."

In 1859, the *Memphis Daily Appeal* featured a series of articles on the highly successful fair in Memphis' rival city of St. Louis. It was pointed out that St. Louis businessmen had large investments in their fair and also received large returns. The paper tried to arouse what it called the "lethargic merchants and real estate owners of Memphis," and urged them to back the fair contests by offering larger monetary premiums. The *Appeal* argued that only then, "will our fair assume an importance worthy of its design; then will thousands of parties contend for the prizes, and many thousands assemble to see the objects worthy of such honors; then will they see and appreciate the importance of our city, and invest their money in our securities." It worked. This practice is still followed today, with Memphis businesses sponsoring many contests at the Mid-South Fair.

Luckily, it took an anonymous contributor who signed his name as "Agricola" to go further than any newspaper or fair official dared go in pointing out

the social and more personal benefits of the fair. Long before video dating and singles bars, Agricola wrote, "Young gentlemen this is the place you may expect to find the one you adore above all others. Old bachelors, this is the place, most probably, you will find one suited to your mind, and, perchance, the means by which your wilderness in life might be speedily curtailed."

With the recreational, financial and social benefits of the fair thus enumerated and explicated, there was one other incentive to increase attendance that Agricultural Society officials resorted to in 1859. The price of admission was reduced from 50 cents to 25 cents. Single carriages were admitted for 50 cents, single buggies for 25 cents, and single persons for 25 cents. Only life members of the Agricultural Society and their families were allowed free admission at the gate.

Pre-Civil War fairs usually began about 9 a.m. and closed at 5 p.m. The period from noon to 2 p.m. was set aside for dinner and relaxation. All announcements were made by the herald, who generally became "perfectly hoarse" long before the events were over. Exhibits were judged and awards made both in the morning and the afternoon. Most of these early fairs lasted five days.

By 1860, the fair finally had become an important fixture in the social and business life of Shelby County. Visitors came from outside Shelby County too. In light of its growing success, the *Daily Argus* newspaper in 1860 made an appeal to Memphis' civic pride as the fair approached: "Let us all prepare then for the enjoyment of the great gala week of the season. Clean up our streets, remove all obstacles from our pavements, furbish our night lamps, open Court Square to the public both day and night, prepare the rostrums, the seats, kettle drums and bells."

The 1860 fair was the most successful one to date. Ten thousand people attended on the final day. Indeed, by then the fair was attracting larger crowds than any other kind of entertainment in the county.

But just as it was gaining support and reaching a position of influence in the region, it was abruptly halted by the Civil War. For the five years of the war there were no fairs, although Confederate soldiers bivouacked at the fairgrounds in 1861 and 1862. And it was not until a few years after the end of the war that Shelby County would attempt to organize another fair.

From War through Yellow Fever Epidemics

The Fairs of 1868 - 1879

When the Shelby County Fair resumed in 1868 it was not set in the same Shelby County which had hosted the highly successful and prosperous 1860 fair eight years earlier. The Civil War had taken its toll. People were still recovering and the lack of participation in the 1868 fair reflected this fact. On the first day of the 1868 fair there were fewer than 200 visitors and not enough entries to award premiums. Moreover, the fair was plagued by rain and mud all week. The schedule called for a three-day run from October 20 to 22. Blaming the poor attendance on the weather, officials decided to add an extra day. Even though many activities were postponed until that last day, attendance was still poor.

The resounding failure of the first post-Civil War fair prompted the officials of the Agricultural Society to regroup and try to find ways to restore the Shelby County Fair to the prominent place in the community it had begun to enjoy before the war. First, the members of the Agricultural Society elected new officers. Then they found a new site for the fair—four miles east of Memphis on the line of the Memphis and Charleston Railroad and adjacent to the race track of the Memphis Jockey Club. That is the location it still occupies today — the present-day Mid-South Fairgrounds.

The Deaderick family originally owned the land where the fairgrounds settled. It had been part of a 5,000-acre plantation which was considered wilderness when Memphis was just starting out in the early 1800s. By 1851, it seemed a little less remote from the city and some of the land was purchased and made into a race track by the Memphis Jockey Club. Horse races were held there in the fall and the spring until the Civil War.

In September of 1869 the *Daily Appeal* reported, "The new fairground, recently purchased, is being fitted for the joint use of the Agricultural Society and the Jockey Club. The fair will begin October 20, and the races will follow in November. A crew of 40 men is engaged in building grandstands to accommodate 1,500 and stables which will be unsurpassed in the country." In addition, two amphitheaters, each with a seating capacity of 3,000, were available on the new site. And separate buildings for housing the mechanical, horticultural and agricultural exhibits were erected.

To the delight of officials, the 1869 fair opened to good weather on October 25 and had a successful six-day run. The premiums awarded for this fair amounted to $10,000, of which the cotton premiums totaled $3,200. There were 109 entries for the grand prize, quoted in the 1869 premium list as $500 for the best bale of cotton. That prize alone was $150 more than the total premiums for the first fair in 1856. The generous prizes for cotton were attributed by the *Memphis Public Ledger* daily newspaper to the good will of local cotton merchants, who wanted to encourage cotton farmers, and to demonstrate "to the country at large the great advantages Memphis enjoys over other cities as a cotton mart."

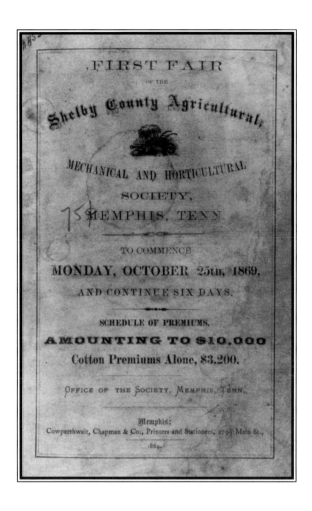

1869 cover of a fair premium list.

tary a red, the treasurer a green and the marshals of the fairgrounds a yellow rosette."

In the culinary department, a jar of peaches which was reported to have been "preserved without sugar or heat" by Memphian A.B. Morrison was of great interest. There was also a stove contest in which the four different competitors baked bread in different stoves for the judges. Awards were determined by the quality of the bread produced, the time required in baking, and the amount of fuel used.

Among the new exhibits in 1869 were various drugs including something called "English Female Bitters." Also of note were the "Louisiana Creole Hair Restorer" and the "Texas Tonic Syrup." Another unusual display was a prize-winning beehive called the "Egyptian Moth Excluding Bee-hive" which received the top prize in its class because "it does really exclude moths." And since the war was not long past, there was a raffle to benefit the Confederate Relief Association, in which the prize was a "handsome silver mounted Montezuma saddle, with its trappings valued at $1,000."

For anyone who has ever attended Memphis or Shelby County schools, the 1870 fair marked the beginning of another cherished tradition which continues today. It was the first year the mayor proclaimed a one-day city holiday at all schools in order for kids to attend the fair.

The Agricultural Society also had decided to expand the fair's scope. This was reflected by its official name, which in 1869 had grown to become "The First Fair of the Shelby County Agricultural, Mechanical and Horticultural Society." The officers of the fair wore "rosettes," or ornamental badges that were color-coded, according to rank, in an attempt to ensure that their prominent status would be recognizable by everyone at the fair. But the code was rather complicated and unless fair-goers continually checked the 1869 schedule of premiums which deciphered it, they would have been hard-pressed to keep track of which color meant what. The president of the society, Enoch Ensley, was to wear a white rosette, "the vice president a white and blue, each member of the board of directors a blue, the secre-

Some other new features appeared during the 1870 fair. Around this time the Shelby County Fairs began to have sideshows which consisted of giants, dwarfs and a few animals, such as monkeys. Another kind of special show of particular note which began in 1870 was the baby show with 27 entries. The Memphis newspaper, *The Daily Avalanche*, reported that a "lucky little lady" who won the top honors was awarded a baby carriage and got wheeled around the arena in it by Colonel J.G. Ballentine, Grand Marshal of the fair "amid the huzzas of the assembled multitude, while the unlucky babies were carried solemnly out of the ring." There were also trotting matches, plowing matches, pigeon-shooting matches, and cow-milking contests in which women participated. One display which attracted a lot of attention was a fan that attached to any chair. According to *The Daily Avalanche*, "you rock, and cool breezes visit you, and flies and mosquitoes *vamose*." The newspaper advised that everybody should have this device.

Even though black people eventually would be banned from participation in the fair with the enactment of the region's "Jim Crow" segregation laws, as late as 1870 black people were still attending the fair and contending for prizes. That year the press reported that "Kate Parker, a colored woman, had crab apple jelly and pickles on display in the Home Made Produce Department" and that "a colored man named Alexander Kennedy" exhibited a dough-kneader.

The 1870 fair became the biggest and best fair the region had ever seen. The premiums were doubled from the year before to $20,000. It all paid off. By opening day there were 300 entries for competition and exhibition. By the end of the week fair officials announced that more than 40,000 people attended the 1870 Shelby County Fair.

The next year was also very successful. The 1871 fair began on October 16 and continued for six days. The main attraction of this year was the appearance of Commodore Mathew Fontaine Maury of Lexington, Virginia, a famous naval officer and scientist who delivered the annual address. He had been a Confederate officer in charge of all coast, harbor and river defenses during the war. By 1871 he had become a professor of meteorology at the Virginia Military Institute. At the fair he spoke on the importance of perfecting ways to predict the weather. This was of great importance to farmers and caused much discussion among his audience.

At the 1872 fair another famous Confederate soldier was in attendance — General Nathan Bedford Forrest. He showed up to watch the horse races and was overheard to say that he had enjoyed them. Many other spectators agreed. The horse races were a big draw at the fairs in the early 1870s. The most popular race

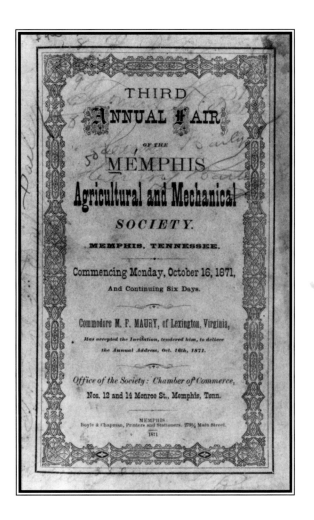

1871 cover of fair program.

was the Peabody Trot. Moreover, baby contests became big hits during this period.

By the early 1870s the annual fair had regained the status and influence it had lost during and immediately after the Civil War. But once again that status was to be put in jeopardy by adverse circumstances. This time it was the yellow fever epidemics that hit Memphis during the decade. Starting in 1873, five attacks of the deadly disease devastated the city. By 1877 it was estimated that more than 22,000 persons had died. Thousands of other citizens had left the city never to return.

There were fairs held in 1873 and 1874, but they were poorly attended. The *Daily Appeal* of October 7, 1874, reported, "The sixth annual fair of the Memphis Agricultural and Mechanical Society commenced yesterday and attendance, we regret to say, was not large. In fact, there were very few visitors on the grounds." By October 10, 1874, the paper announced that, "Mayor Loague, the Cotton Exchange and Chamber of Commerce have issued a proclamation suggesting that all places of business in Memphis be closed today and that the public at large — black and white, clerk, merchant and mechanic — unite in a demonstration to sustain our Agricultural Society and make it worthy of Shelby County."

Just as it had done in 1859, the daily paper pointed to the success of the fair in St. Louis as an incentive to instill some competitive civic pride, and motivate the people to support the Shelby County fair. The report went on to say, "This will be the third day of our fair . . . . We regret to say the first two days were poorly attended. If we are to thrive like St. Louis, we must do like St. Louis. We must support our basic farming interests or our commerce will never prosper. Let Memphis throng to the Fairgrounds today." But such pleas did little to draw citizens to the fairs. Even though a scaled-down fair continued through the 1870s, the yellow fever epidemics and resulting economic depression threatened to halt the annual event altogether.

Post Yellow Fever

The Fair from 1880 - 1906

The period from 1880 to 1906 was a time of rebuilding for Memphis. The few fairs held during those years never gained the momentum they needed to once again grow into sustained annual events. Still, they did continue to perpetuate some of the traditions established just before and after the Civil War. Mainly, though, the fairgrounds were used for horse racing through most of that 26-year period.

In 1880 and 1881, fairs were sponsored by the Shelby County Grange Association and held at the same

fairgrounds location. Public interest was low. In 1882, Col. Henry A. Montgomery organized the New Memphis Jockey Club and purchased the old mile-long race track and surrounding fairgrounds, naming it Montgomery Park. In 1885, the Jockey Club purchased more land and extended the site from the railroad tracks north to Central Avenue.

Although it is not known if the following story is completely true, legend has it that Col. Montgomery died suddenly while giving a speech at the racing park that carried his name. Reportedly, he left the Tennessee Club downtown on October 20, 1887, and went in his horse-drawn carriage to his home at Poplar and Bellevue and then on out to the Montgomery Park Jockey Club. There, he took part in a "tallyho" — a kind of fox hunt. He drove four chestnut horses and all the while complained to a companion that his brakes were not working and his arms were tired from the exertion of controlling the horses. But upon finishing the tallyho and arriving back at the club, he persevered and delivered a brief but eloquent welcome address to the Western Waterways convention which was in session there. Immediately upon conclusion of his remarks he collapsed and was carried from the podium and pronounced dead by a doctor. His name lived on, however, as the park grew to become one of the premier horse racing venues in the country during the next two decades.

The 1880s and 1890s saw saddle-horse racing and harness racing become main events of a regular racing season at Montgomery Park. The Tennessee Derby was established and held at Montgomery Park through these years. With a large purse, it was one of the major horse racing events in the country. In fact, it was apparently more famous than the Kentucky Derby at the turn of the century. In 1899, papers reported that the entire Tennessee legislature attended opening day at Montgomery Park, "almost to a man."

In 1890 and 1891 fairs also were held at Montgomery Park. The biggest attractions at these early 1890s fairs were the ceremonies honoring Confederate soldiers. But in 1893 and 1894 the fairs were moved to a site in North Memphis called Billings Park, which, in due course, would become a rival racing venue to Montgomery Park. After 1893 the annual fairs were to disappear from the county for many years. Very small-scale merchant fairs were held downtown in 1899 and 1900, but they were mainly street fairs.

In 1905 the Tennessee legislature outlawed pari-mutuel betting and both Montgomery Park and the Memphis Driving Park (formerly Billings Park) were forced to curtail their racing seasons. Around that same time, Memphis was getting back on firmer financial footing. After the demise of horse racing, fairs again became popular as a way to promote the economic interests of the Memphis area, especially after St. Louis hosted its successful 1904 World's Fair.

The fact that in 1906 city leaders mounted a new Shelby County Fair must have been due, at least in part, to Memphis' ongoing rivalry with St. Louis. And the success of that year's fair led to the idea of reviving the annual festival and making it a major regional event for the whole Mid-South.

In the early 1900s the Business Men's Club was founded to promote investment in Memphis. Its members therefore became natural partners with the city in the effort to revive an annual fair. By 1907 they were talking of forming an organization to manage the annual fair for the benefit of the agricultural interests in Memphis and the surrounding area. And by January of 1908 the Tri-State Fair Association was born.

Local businessman Frederick Orgill was elected the first president of the association. With a total capital of $50,000, its shares of stock, or "subscriptions" as they were called, were sold for $100 each and were limited to five shares per person. The businessmen of Memphis bought up the entire amount and strongly supported the association.

The first task of the association was to find a suitable location for the new fair. Organizers favored the site of the old Memphis Jockey Club at the old Montgomery Park horse-racing course. For a few years, owners of the track had hoped that the betting laws would be rescinded. But by 1908 it was apparent that the track could never again function as it had in its glory days. At the same time, the Tri-State Fair Association needed grounds that were suitable for the events and crowds of the proposed fair. Since other fairs traditionally had been held at that location over the years, and the grandstand and some of the other structures there were still in good shape, it was the logical choice. So in the spring of 1908 the association took out a five-year lease on the grounds.

Montgomery Park, the former gathering place of the upper echelons of Memphis society, became a hotbed of coordinated activity. Renovation and construction continued through the summer. On a Sunday morning in August 1908 *The Commercial Appeal* enticed readers with a description of the newly fitted fairgrounds:

> *When the three large entrance gates to the Tri-State Fair are thrown wide on Sept. 28, thousands of Memphians will open their eyes in wonder at the complete metamorphosis that has taken place within a few months at historic old Montgomery Park.*

The newspaper article went on to describe how the old racing track, "where thousands of dollars have been lost and won in the days gone by," had become part of, "the most complete fair grounds ever built in the South." Not only were the grounds intended to be used for the fair, but the old Memphis Jockey Club clubhouse was to be made into the Tri-State Club which was to serve as a country club throughout the year. *The Commercial Appeal* explained:

> *It is expected that by the last of this year [1908] the club will have its full maximum of 2,000 members, who will constitute just that many boosters for the fair. The clubhouse is now being fitted up with all the accessories to be found in the modern country club. Lounging rooms, a library, billiard rooms, dining rooms, grill rooms and bath rooms are some of the features planned for the club. In addition there are golf links, tennis and baseball grounds, all of which will be open to club members all through the year.*

To house the exhibits at the fair, a number of new buildings were added to the grounds including, "a manufacturer's hall, an implement hall, a vehicle hall and a pure food hall." The largest new building on the fairgrounds was the exhibit hall in which "the displays of merchants and the handiwork of women" would be exhibited.

In 1908 a local periodical called *The Journal of Commerce* described the upcoming Tri-State Fair as "a wonderful exposition of the varied products of the South, embracing livestock, agriculture, poultry, woman's work, etc." And when the fair opened, it proved to be an apt description. There were culinary contests and other agricultural contests, as well as horse shows and dog shows. The first hog show was held that year and praised by the journal as one of "the best shows of the kind ever had in this section of the country."

While livestock and farming concerns along with the exhibits and competitions were the undisputed centerpieces of the Tri-State Fair, organizers also added attractions strictly for the entertainment of fair-goers. The old race track came into good use for pony racing, mule racing and harness racing, as well as some auto racing and motorcycle racing, all of which were popular attractions. It turns out that a loophole in the racing laws said betting on horses could continue if the profits benefitted a charity. So racing did continue and, one year, the beneficiary of the events was even a local church.

1908 marked the first time Memphis had a midway at its fair. Among midway attractions that year were the living half-woman, half-alligator, and the headless man. Other entertainment included high wire acts, trapeze artists, balloon races and parachute leaps.

New "special days" were featured. The 1908 fair's opening day was Governor's Day, and the governors of all three states — Tennessee, Mississippi, and Arkansas — appeared. Governor Patterson of Tennessee made the keynote speech, stressing the importance of fairs in educating people and increasing their camaraderie. Other special days through the ten-day run of the fair included Farmers' Union Day, Traveling Man's Day and, of course, Children's Day when all school-aged kids got a day off to attend the fair. On Children's Day a pony, Little Ben, was given away to Lindstedt Whitemore, aged 14, for holding the coupon with the lucky prize-winning number. The boy lived at 288 Union Avenue, then a residential area, but there is no explanation as to whether he was expected to keep the pony at his home.

This post card shows how the fairgrounds looked in 1908. Note that none of the land in the foreground, west of the fairgrounds, had been developed yet.

Although all the buildings of the fair were closed on Sunday, a band from Italy called Ricci's Imperial Italian Band gave a concert of sacred music. There was also an airship, as it was called, in which Professor Thomas Baldwin amazed the crowds with his daily flights. This was only five years after the Wright brothers had first flown at Kitty Hawk, North Carolina, and Captain Baldwin's airship looked more like a modern-day blimp than the flying machines of that day. Still, witnessing this "aeronaut" in action was one of the first experiences Memphians had with manned flight.

All in all, the first Tri-State Fair of 1908 was a success in exhibits, entertainment and attendance. It inherited some of the traditions of earlier Shelby County fairs, but it also gave birth to new traditions and set the precedent upon which all the successive fairs in Memphis were to be modeled. In its basic intent and character, the 1908 fair was a direct predecessor to the current Mid-South Fair. Memphis was beginning to take its place among the important urban areas in the country and the fair was a way the city could bring together the urban and rural, the merchant and farmer of this region.

Nevertheless, the first Tri-State Fair lost money. In response, the Fair Association redoubled its efforts and increased the capital stock for the 1909 fair to $100,000. Again, the businessmen of the city showed their faith in the venture by quickly buying up the additional $50,000 worth of stock. Most people felt the fair had great potential for eventual financial success.

The 1909 fair ran for 12 days, from September 28 through October 9. In the introduction to the program that year the organizers cited the achievements of the first Tri-State Fair, and promised that the second would continue the tradition of annually showing the people of the three states "an immense growing institution wherein modern methods of soil cultivation, improved livestock breeding and everything of interest and benefit to the farmer, planter and his family will be brought together, exhibited and lessons by comparison will be taught." The association also promised that "the entertainment will be clean, moral and free from all objectionable features."

On the streets, personal safety was an important concern in Memphis in the early part of the 20th century because the city had the dubious distinction of having one of the highest crime rates in the country and the highest murder rate per capita of any U.S. city. No doubt with this in mind the authors of the 1909 program assured fair-goers that, "good order will be preserved, and ladies and children, especially, can feel perfectly safe at all times in all parts of the grounds and buildings."

Once again the agricultural and livestock exhibits and competitions lived up to their billing. The program claimed that "every breed of beef and dairy cattle, sheep and hogs will be represented with their best specimens, many of which will be for sale, and should find their way to the farms of the Tri-State farmers." There was also a show of mules and donkeys, and a poultry show, which the Tri-State Poultry Association said would be the largest show of its kind ever in the South. The Woman's Department continued to offer awards for food and handiwork including a two-dollar first prize for handsomest sofa pillow, a two-dollar first prize for daintiest baby cap, and a one-dollar first prize for best one dozen button holes.

The entertainment and diversions were similar to the year before with harness racing, an airship, balloon races, and a high wire act by "James Hardy the High Wire King." At night, fair-goers were dazzled by a spectacle called, "The Battle in the Clouds — the greatest display of fireworks ever attempted in this country." And at the race track there was even a motorcycle meet for amateurs and professionals of the Southern states sponsored by the Memphis Motor Cycle Club.

The 1909 midway had 20 shows. In addition, fair-goers could see free acts such as Rube Shields — "the funny man who makes people laugh," Dakota Dan's Wild West show, and Spellman's Performing Bears. These bears rode bicycles, walked a rope, rode in automobiles, tried to talk and, in short, did "everything" — at least according to their advertisements.

LARGEST SHOW

EVER!

The 1909 fair was once again a big success in terms of its exhibits and entertainment, but just as it had the year before, the fair lost money. Businessmen made up the balance, and the 450 stockholders were satisfied the fair was still a solid venture. Their faith was merited because by 1910 the fair began to find firmer financial ground.

The year 1910 also was a milestone in the political history of Memphis. That was the year E. H. Crump, who came to be known as "Boss Crump" because of his machine-style politics, took office as mayor of the city. Crump actually served as mayor for only a few years, from 1910 until 1915. In 1940 he served again for five minutes in a political maneuver in which he was elected and resigned immediately, replacing himself with his hand-picked candidate. But despite the fact that he was mayor for a relatively short time all together, he wielded so much power and influence that his word and will would dominate Memphis politics virtually until his death in 1954.

For the Mid-South Fair, 1910 marked the beginning of another reign which would also last many years. State Senator Frank Fuller became the secretary/manager of the Tri-State Fair that year and would keep that position, running all the successive fairs, through to the 1938 Mid-South Fair. In the 1910s Fuller and Crump did a lot to ensure that the Tri-State Fair would become a permanent fixture in the city of Memphis.

The fairgrounds was also the setting for yet another milestone in Memphis history in 1910. In April, a four-day National Aviation Meet was held there. It was one of the city's first chances to see the new flying machine people had heard so much about. The grandstand was packed to watch the numerous flights, and a few crashes — three to be exact. Fortunately, no one was seriously injured in any of them. This meet was the kind of event that made Memphians begin to see the fairgrounds as an invaluable year-round part of the city's park system.

The fair itself was evolving into an attraction for out-of-town visitors as well. The Commercial Appeal reported that before the opening of the 1910 fair, "every hotel in the city had all the patrons that they could comfortably accommodate." And the needs of tourists to the fair that year were taken care of better than ever before. A periodical called The Southern Farm Advocate ran an article in its Sept. 1, 1910, issue titled "Comfort and Convenience at the Tri-State Fair." The article cited the care fair officials had taken in providing for fair-goers' comfort:

> Rest rooms and such like conveniences for both ladies and gentlemen have been materially improved, these changes have included the installation of modern toilet rooms in accessible locations and a barbershop in charge of competent help. A public service building will contain a post office, telephone exchange ... an information bureau. While good pure ice water will be found on every hand. In short, while visitors are learning facts that will mean money to them in their regular occupations or are indulging in wholesome recreation that the fair will afford, they will at the same time be made comfortable.

At the fair of 1910 a new emphasis was placed on education, and one side of the Agricultural building was dedicated to educational exhibits. Ladies' Day was added to the list of special days at the fair in 1910. There was also a proliferation of artwork on display that year. So much, in fact, that the fair management began to consider constructing a separate building just for the display of artwork entries. This led to the formation of a fair committee headed by Mrs. Ben M. Bruce, the superintendent of the woman's department since the first Tri-State Fair in 1908, which began a campaign to raise money for a permanent art museum. The core of the museum's permanent collection was to be taken from the fair's art exhibits. Eventually, park commissioners agreed to apportion land in Overton Park for the museum. The Brooks Memorial Art Gallery was built there in 1916, and it did display art from the fair, providing yet another example of how the fair has contributed to the development of Memphis.

A dedication marker denotes the year the Fairgrounds Park was purchased in 1912.

The fair also continually paralleled the tenor of the times and social mores of the region. In 1896 the well-known, landmark Supreme Court case of Plessy vs. Ferguson had made racial segregation legal if "separate but equal" facilities were provided for both races. Therefore, fairs in the South were segregated, and the Tri-State and Mid-South Fairs were no exception. Because of this, there was little hope of reviving the early tradition of black participation in Shelby County fairs.

In 1911, African-Americans organized their own fair called the Negro Tri-State Fair. It ran at the fairgrounds for a few days after the white fair. Some of the same acts and attractions would stay over from the white event to take part in this fair. But the Negro Tri-State Fair had separate management. It was founded by a prominent African-American physician named L.G. Patterson, and run by African-American leaders. When the white fair later became known as the Mid-South Fair the black fair became simply the Tri-State Fair. It became an important event in the African-American community for many decades until it was discontinued in 1959. Shortly thereafter, the Mid-South Fair once again became a unified event when it was integrated in 1962.

Through the 1910s the Tri-State Fair grew, becoming an ever more established part of the annual Memphis calendar. In 1912 the city bought Montgomery Park from the Jockey Club, which had leased it to the Fair association. Mayor Crump engineered the sale. The city paid $250,000 and placed the 119 acres under the jurisdiction of the Recreation Park Commission for development as a place for public amusement and recreation. Although a few renovations to the grounds took place in 1912, major renovations were planned for five years down the road.

Meanwhile, the city used its newly owned fair grounds in 1912 as a refugee camp for black victims of the huge flood that hit the area that year. Black refugees from the lowlands of Arkansas and Mississippi were cared for at "Camp Crump" for six weeks in April.

One major theme of the Mid-South Fair has always been the importance of keeping up with new trends in agriculture. The Memphis Commission Government continued to stress that theme when it preached diversification of crops in 1913:

"Memphis, as we all know, is the center of a great agricultural empire, and the continued growth and prosperity of the city is inseparably linked with agricultural pursuits. In the Memphis territory cotton has from time immemorial been king and will probably continue to be for all time, but those who closely observe the trend of the times know that the South is on the threshold of a new era, which will bring about a diversification of crops and the growing of live stock. ..." The 1913 fair will see these ideas more fully elaborated than ever before.

Yet, mindful of the fact that Memphis was also an urban area, the promoters went on to say that, "the fair management, realizing that all work and no play makes Jack a dull boy, has provided an amusement program to suit the tastes of all ... and the visitor to whom the agricultural side of the fair does not appeal will find much to occupy his time."

This engraving beckoned visitors to the 1913 Tri-State Fair.

The fairs of 1914, 1915 and 1916 all continued to echo these themes. In 1914 another special day, Suffrage Day, was added to the fair in an ongoing attempt to present innovative ideas to the public. A fair brochure that year said, "No matter what one may individually think of Woman's Suffrage, the cause has many sincere advocates among men as well as women, and is bound to eventually triumph in America. The Fair, being an exponent of progressive ideas, is glad to welcome the women on Wednesday ... when special exercises will be held on the grounds both day and night. Speakers of note will be present to address those interested."

Besides the latest political and agricultural trends fair-goers were also exposed to the latest dance crazes. The 1914 brochure described one of its vaudeville acts this way:

"The new dances have taken the country by storm and every one is either learning the Tango, Maxixe or Hesitation, ... and no vaudeville program of today is considered complete without a dancing number. For the Fair we have booked King and Jolie, who have the reputation of being particularly pleasing and skillful in their expositions of the dancing craze."

Also, a promotional brochure justified the new automobile races at the fair this way: "The American

A crowd at the grandstand and clubhouse during the 1916 Tri-State Fair.

public demands for its entertainment that which will excite and thrill as only professional automobile racing can."

By 1915, the fair had become self-supporting, with any profits going back into fairground improvements. Senator Fuller gained appropriations from the Tennessee legislature for supplementing the agriculture exhibit premiums. Meanwhile, fair officials had begun to clamor for larger facilities. In 1916 the county gave $15,000 for construction of a Shelby County Building (a forerunner to the current building with that name) and a total renovation of the grounds was planned. However, two events combined to stall those plans.

In 1915 Mayor Crump had been ousted from office in a scandal surrounding the lack of enforcement of state prohibition laws in Memphis. Two years later the U.S. became a participant in World War I. The uncertainty these two events created in Memphis politics and the world delayed any renovation project. The war put a damper on fair attendance that first

Horses before a harness race at the race track in 1916.

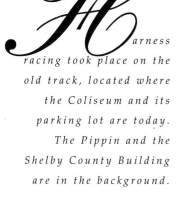

*H*arness *racing took place on the old track, located where the Coliseum and its parking lot are today. The Pippin and the Shelby County Building are in the background.*

year. But the fair was not cancelled and the military even used it as an opportunity to recruit soldiers. By 1918 the U.S. government had extensive exhibits at the fair.

In 1918 an auto show was added. Also that year more than $1.3 million worth of livestock — mainly hogs and cattle — were exhibited at the fair. This all meant that fair officials had a strong case for more barns and for expansion of the facilities. In 1917 the Tennessee Legislature abolished the Recreation Park Commission which had been in charge of developing the fairgrounds and put the grounds under the auspices of the Memphis Park Commission. In 1918 a plan was drawn up to improve the grounds. All agreed the first step in that effort would be to shorten the old one-mile race track, making it into a half-mile track, and making way for new buildings and an amusement park.

Winning public support for the plan and securing the money to implement expansion of the fair was the mission of fair officials for the next year or so. Calling livestock "the soul of the Tri-State Fair," S. M. Neely, one of the revived fair's 1908 founders, made the case for more barns to house the annual influx of cattle, swine and sheep in a 1919 issue of the Memphis Chamber of Commerce Journal. He told of the $25,000 in livestock premiums alone that the fair was now awarding, and he went on to boost the idea of total fairgrounds renovation:

> *The future of the Tri-State Fair seems exceedingly brilliant. Its success has been achieved and its patronage is growing each year. ... But the time has come when a broader foundation must be provided for the future growth of the fair. Their grounds must be rearranged. The small exhibit halls must give way to larger and more substantial buildings*

that will house the agricultural products and livestock of the rapidly developing tri-state area.

The Tri-State Fair is no longer an experiment. It is a demonstrated success. It can and will become one of America's greatest fairs. ... It started as a Memphis enterprise and has become a regional institution. It merits the support of all who would see this territory become the richest agricultural region in the world.

The next three years were to see the realization of that plea. In 1920, $100,000 was spent on shortening the race track, moving the grandstand, and undertaking some related construction projects. The new half-mile race track was at the southern end of the fairgrounds where the Coliseum and its parking lot are now.

To the north, where the old track had extended for another half mile, the grounds were being prepared for many new buildings; one exhibit hall was completed that year with more to come. Moreover, the area to the west and north of the new track was being made ready for the installation of an amusement park.

By 1922 much of the building work was completed. A Memphis Chamber of Commerce Journal article surmised that the 1922 fair visitor "will be convinced that only Aladdin could have wrought the miraculous changes that will be seen on every hand at the Memphis fairgrounds." All together, more than $500,000 was

The Shelby County Building that still stands today was built in 1922.

spent on new buildings and additional space. The city purchased an additional 26 1/2 acres "adjoining the fairgrounds and fronting on Central Avenue." This land was initially used for additional parking, since more and more Memphians were traveling to the fair in automobiles.

Before the 1922 fair began, a grand, new municipal swimming pool was opened on the grounds in the summer. It was already a huge success by fair time since some 80,000 people had tested its waters during the first 30 days of its operation. Despite immediate popularity, the new pool wasn't well-received by everyone in the city. In fact, the Shelby County Baptist Association, shocked that men and women were being allowed to swim during the same hours, and that women were wearing tight-fitting, immodest bathing suits, called the pool "a veritable hellhole." But such behavior was obviously not curtailed by protest, since the Memphis Chamber of Commerce Journal reported that the pool was expected to be "a big amusement feature of fair week."

To the north of the race track, a new Woman's Building was constructed in 1922. Just east of it, a new agricultural hall was built and dubbed, "the behemoth of the new array." The colossal structure was built of ornamental brick and terra cotta after a Spanish design. Today this building is still standing and is called the Shelby County Building.

Also added to the grounds were the new livestock buildings for which fair officials had long pleaded. These included a new cattle barn and a new swine barn, both of which could also accommodate sheep and other livestock. To top it all off, new roads and walkways were constructed through the fairgrounds, and an attractive new entrance gate was put up on the western side of the grounds off of East Parkway. The final phase of the fairgrounds renovation was completed in time for the 1923 fair. A "joy plaza," or amusement park, was installed along the western rim of the grounds bordering East Parkway. Two enduring landmarks of the fairgrounds also were erected in this year — the Zippin Pippin roller coaster and the Grand Carousel merry-go-round.

The Grand Carousel also traveled far and wide before it landed at the fairgrounds to merrily go round and round from 1923 on. It was built in Chicago in 1909 by Gustav Dentzel, a member of a famous carousel-making family. Its original cost was $15,000. After a time in Philadelphia it finally ended up in Memphis. Other featured attractions of the new amusement park were the Old Mill ride, a shooting gallery, a ride called the Whip, another called the Kentucky Derby, an airplane swing, and a house of mystery. The new "joy plaza" was to stay in operation throughout the summer months.

With all of this renovation, and the end of World War I, the fairs of the early twenties began drawing unparalleled crowds. Nearly 200,000 attended the 1923 Tri-State Fair. Yet, despite this expansion, the fairs still remained true to their original purpose of educating and entertaining farmers and the city folk alike. Entertainment during that time included beauty contests and historical pageants, such as a 1920 program called "The Path of Progress" which commemorated the 300th anniversary of the pilgrims landing at Plymouth Rock. The midway continued showing "every sort of fun and freak palace." Harness racing and auto races were also big attractions, as was the poultry and pigeon show. A horse show was added in 1924.

The exhibits and educational presentations of the fair became more prominent during these years. In 1922 an exhibit called the Cotton Temple displayed a

Cotton Temple built like a log cabin.

This is the earliest available picture of the Pippin. The new 1912 Ford shows the roller coaster was built around that time.

THE PIPPIN HAD BEEN MOVED FROM ITS ORIGINAL LOCATION AT THE EAST END AMUSEMENT PARK ON MADISON WEST OF OVERTON SQUARE. IT HAS BEEN OFFICIALLY DATED BACK TO AT LEAST 1915, BUT A PICTURE OF EAST END PARK IN 1912 SHOWS THE PIPPIN IN THE BACKGROUND. WHEN IT WAS INSTALLED AT THE FAIRGROUNDS, ITS CONFIGURATION WAS CHANGED INTO A FIGURE-EIGHT SHAPE. TODAY, THE COASTER STILL OPERATES AS ONE OF THE OLDEST ROLLER COASTERS IN THE COUNTRY, AND CERTAINLY ONE OF THE OLDEST WOODEN ROLLER COASTERS IN THE WORLD.

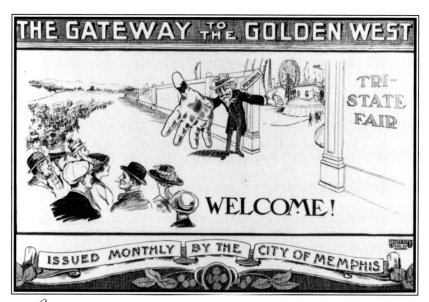

Another engraving promoting the Tri-State Fair in 1924.

full-size structure, assembled like a log cabin, but made entirely of cotton bales. Even the roof was cotton. In 1924 the fair saw some of its first butter statuary. On display were scenes of dairies, including a life-size cow, all sculpted from frozen butter.

In 1923 WMC radio and The Commercial Appeal newspaper had a special "radio-phone receiving set" in the Shelby County Building on which they could receive concerts from all stations in the country. The newspaper assured its readers that "a competent staff of experts will be there to tune in on Chicago, Los Angeles and a hundred other points."

Some educational and promotional information was imparted through the newest technology, called "motion picture machines." These machines showed free movies. One such movie which was particularly popular took viewers on a tour of the Ford automobile plants.

An interesting talk was given in 1923 under the auspices of the woman's department. A brochure said that at two o'clock one afternoon there would be a lecture on "The Art of Corsetry." But in parenthesis it warned that the presentation was "(for women only)." Also sponsored by the women's department that year were some unusual contests, including a decorated tables competition in which the "best arranged and most artistically decorated tables" in two classes — professional and amateur — would be awarded the first prizes of $20 each.

By 1924, admission to the fair was 75 cents, and $40,000 in premiums were being awarded, including $18,000 for horse and auto races. By 1926 the auto show was exhibiting $250,000 worth of new cars. At the same time, the theme of crop diversification and the mission of encouraging better farming techniques continued to be promoted throughout the 1920s. Of course, politicians still maintained a presence. In 1923 Tennessee Governor Austin Peay visited the fair on Tennessee Day. A new special day was added in 1924 — Grandmothers' Day.

The early twenties saw the boys' and girls' agricultural clubs, sponsored by the federal government, take on prominence at the fair. There were camps and special competitions for young male and female farmers from all over the Mid-South. These groups later evolved into the Future Farmers of America and Future Homemakers of America.

The 1927 and 1928 Tri-State Fairs were the largest fairs ever held in the region at that time. This was mainly due to the fact that they were also the setting for the National Dairy Exposition. The 1927 fair and dairy expo played host to a world record holder for butter production— a cow named Daisy Aagie Ormsby III, who produced 33,140 pounds of milk and more than 1,607 pounds of butter in a year. It was quite a coup for Memphis to host the dairy exposition since the show had never been held in the South, which was not noted for its dairy production. However, the arrangement proved mutually beneficial for both parties since the 1927 National Dairy Exposition in Memphis was the most successful in the show's 21-year history. And the 1927 fair had the highest attendance of any Tri-State Fair to date with more than 275,000 attending. With all that success it was a natural for the Tri-State Fair to ask the Dairy Expo to come back to Memphis the following year, an invitation which National Dairy officials gladly accepted.

The National Cotton Show was added to the fair in 1928. Organized along the same lines as the National Dairy Show, the cotton show was sponsored by Sears & Roebuck and the National Fertilizer Association. The aim was to show cotton products and to promote the agriculture and industry surrounding cotton production.

Thus, the official name for the 1928 fair was "The Twenty-First Annual Exhibition of the National Dairy Exposition held at the Twentieth Annual Tri-State Fair and in combination with the First Annual National Cotton Show." Perhaps it was the length of that name which spurred fair officials to rethink how they titled the event altogether. The fair had grown by leaps and bounds in the previous decade, and its entries and scope now encompassed more than the tri-state area. So, in conjunction with the Evening Appeal newspaper, the fair held a contest to find a new name. A woman named Daisy Hinton came up with the more succinct "Mid-South Fair and Dairy Show" and won $65 for her winning suggestion.

A well-known Memphian named Lloyd T. Binford took on the presidency of the fair in 1928. It was in that same year that he also became chairman of the Board of Censors. He was in charge of determining what was proper and improper in films and was responsible for banning many films in Memphis. As his reputation grew, his word on films became as good as law throughout the South. The job of chief censor was a Boss Crump-approved political appointment, and obviously Crump continued to approve of Binford's work, because while he was president of the fair for a respectable length of time — four years — he remained chief of censors for 28 years. However, in 1928 his influence on popular culture had not yet been felt. And as the fair headed into 1929, it was in the best shape it had ever been. It had a new name, prominence in the community and in the nation, and a strong, well-connected leader. Officially incorporated as the Mid-South Fair, its future seemed limitless.

The National Cotton Show made its first appearance in 1928 at the Tri-State Fair.

Three

The Mid-South Fair
1929 — 1993

MID-SOUTH FAIR - 1930S AND 1940S

In mid-October 1929, all was well and proceeding as planned. The leaves were turning on the trees of Memphis and the first newly named Mid-South Fair had come and gone with great success. At the fairgrounds, officials were pleased with the final attendance figure of 185,425. Minus the Dairy Show, they had expected the numbers to drop. But the figures remained nearly 18,000 higher that year than the attendance of 167,781 at the 1926 fair, the last fair held without the added attraction of the National Dairy Show.

Late in October 1929, the calm and contentment of that fall were broken, when, on October 29, the stock market crashed. Suddenly America, and much of the rest of world, was thrown into economic turmoil. For the next several years almost no one or no thing was immune to the effects of the Great Depression, including the Mid-South Fair. The limitless potential that officials had envisioned for the fair in the roaring twenties was definitely obscured. In 1930, just a year after the crash, fair attendance dropped to around 152,000, the lowest it had been in nine years. It was to go lower still in the next few years. During the early thirties mere survival was a struggle for the Mid-South Fair, just as it was for many Mid-Southerners.

*D*espite the downturn, some plans initiated before the Depression were realized. In 1930, two important new buildings were completed on the fairgrounds. One was the Casino, which was independently owned and built at a cost of $100,000. This Casino had nothing to do with gambling; it was strictly a dance hall. At the time, the term "casino" merely meant a hall used for social amusements. This attractive round building boasted a $15,000 maple dance floor, inlaid with oak and rosewood, with what was called a "celotex" cushion underneath, which reportedly made dancing on it "a dream to remember." Suspended from its ceiling was a glittering crystal reflector, a forerunner of the reflecting balls that later hung in most discos during the 1970s. Fairview Junior High School also went up in 1930. Built by the city, it still stands at the northwest corner of the fairgrounds.

*H*andbills from famous orchestras that performed at the Casino ballroom.

In 1931 the fair had a deficit of $4,200. The declining attendance due to hard times probably had something to do with that. But at the time, the loss of income was blamed on the abuse of free tickets, which fair Manager Frank Fuller said had "developed into a racket." The fair lost an estimated $10,000 that year because so many people got free passes, then turned around and gave them to others to reuse. The problem

A homemakers' exhibit was an indication of the Depression taking hold at the 1931 Mid-South Fair. A sign talks of "hard times" and another warns, "every idle minute is a sin against time."

The latest models of refrigerators displayed at the 1931 fair.

was corrected in 1932 just in time for the fair's attendance to hit rock bottom at around 95,000, the lowest it had been for at least 20 years. Hard times were everywhere, but the fair persevered; it had survived adversity before and it would survive again.

In 1933, Herbert Hoover left office and America had a new president, Franklin D. Roosevelt. People started to believe things could get better. At the Mid-South Fair they did. In 1934 the fair again started to show a profit, which it used in turn to repay its debts. That favorable circumstance would continue for three more years, until the fair was finally in the black again in 1937.

Events at the Mid-South Fair during the thirties were similar to those of the twenties, except on a smaller scale. There were no special national exhibitions like the National Dairy Show. But the fair continued to appeal to both the rural and urban dwellers of the Mid-South by featuring the usual mix of agricultural and entertainment attractions. It continued to present contests, competitions and exhibits. Auto races were increasingly popular, and the daredevil "hell drivers" of the thirties drew especially big crowds to the grandstand.

Although life was tough for almost everybody during the Depression, the fair did its best to keep a light touch. Some of its unique features probably helped take fair-goers' minds off their worries. In 1930 there was a wedding held at the midway on the final day of the fair. In 1934 the Service Ice Company exhibit featured a human polar bear named "Freezo." Daily he would get into a 1,400-pound, ice "coffin," wearing only an ordinary swim suit, and remain inside for an hour. This stunt was so well-attended that the crush of the crowds almost overturned Freezo's "coffin." A few days into the fair, a microphone from the WREC radio station was frozen into the block of ice with Freezo, and the local papers reported that "the first broadcast from a cake of ice was staged." Freezo explained that he shivered the whole time to keep his blood from coagulating, and controlled his breathing. "As for the cold," said Freezo, "why, that can never be any less or more than 32 degrees Fahrenheit." In real life, Freezo was a Memphis boy named Elton Rogers who had been performing this amazing stunt for a few years for vaudeville audiences nationwide. In 1932, he had showed it at the World's Fair in Chicago.

And if that were not enough, another attraction of the 1934 fair was the appearance of "Jadaan," the Arabian horse which had been ridden by silent-film star Rudolph Valentino in his famous 1921 movie *The Sheik.* Riding Jadaan at the fair was an unidentified man wearing the same clothing Valentino, the silent screen's greatest lover, had worn in his picture *The Son of the Sheik,* one of the silver screen's earliest sequels.

Throughout the thirties Hollywood was becoming a more prevalent force in the culture of the U.S., a fact reflected in its growing presence among the attractions of the Mid-South Fair. But without television and the kind of press coverage entertainment news gets today, the trappings of Hollywood success were still rather unfamiliar to most of America. In 1935 for instance, a new and exciting exhibit at the upcoming fair was announced this way in *The Commercial Appeal* — without any mention of the name "Oscar":

> *Woman's accomplishments in the motion picture field will be further emphasized during the Mid-South Fair by the display, for two one-hour periods daily, of the gold award presented to Claudette Colbert by the Motion Picture Academy of Arts and Sciences. . . . The award, a 17-inch gold statue, is similar to others made annually at Hollywood in the various fields of the industry for the most outstanding work of the year. Miss Colbert won this special recognition for her work in the picture "It Happened One Night."*

While lack of the kind of total media coverage that brings all corners of the world into our homes today meant that news traveled more slowly, and less widely, problems in handling public relations and image could still be challenges for many in the public eye. This was brought out when newspaper editors from the Mid-South were invited to a luncheon with fair officials and the governor of Tennessee in 1936.

Governor Browning obviously felt the Mid-South Fair had an especially important mission in boost-

ing the profile of the area. He urged the editors to work harder to spread the word about the "rich natural resources and the great agricultural and industrial activity" of Tennessee and the region, instead of dwelling on what he called "incidentals." He said that when he traveled outside of Tennessee he was constantly asked about these more infamous and unflattering incidentals such as child brides in the state, or the Dayton, Tennessee, "monkey trial." (He was referring to the famous Scopes Monkey Trial of 1925 in which a teacher was tried and convicted for teaching the theory of evolution in the public schools.) The governor stressed how much institutions like the Mid-South Fair can do to promote the agricultural advancement of the Mid-South territory, and emphasized how important it was to the region that such accomplishments be publicized and recognized.

The quest for ways to promote the benefits of the fair to the region continued in 1936 and 1937 since the fair's contract with the city for use of the fairgrounds was to expire in December 1937. The slogan selected for the 1936 fair was "where education, agriculture and industry meet." It was a boost to the public profile of the fair that, by then, it was a meeting place for participants from at least eight states: Tennessee, Arkansas, Mississippi, Missouri, Kentucky, Louisiana, Alabama and Oklahoma.

The fair began to grow again, too. Its first real championship contest rodeo was held in 1936. Until then, there had been rodeo events at the fair, but never had fair-goers been offered a program of what was called, "Real Cowboy Contests." This new event was said to be the first and only contest rodeo ever held south of the Ohio River and east of the Mississippi River. The fair offered $2,400 in cash prizes that year for contestants. Also in 1936, the coronation ball for the new queen of the annual beauty contest became a little classier when, for the first time, it was held in the swank Casino ballroom on the first night of the fair.

UNTIL THEN, THERE HAD BEEN RODEO EVENTS AT THE FAIR, BUT NEVER HAD FAIR-GOERS BEEN OFFERED A PROGRAM OF WHAT WAS CALLED, "REAL COWBOY CONTESTS." THIS NEW EVENT WAS SAID TO BE THE FIRST AND ONLY CONTEST RODEO EVER HELD SOUTH OF THE OHIO RIVER AND EAST OF THE MISSISSIPPI RIVER. THE FAIR OFFERED $2,400 IN CASH PRIZES THAT YEAR FOR CONTESTANTS.

The city continued to use the fairgrounds year-round. Between the 1936 and 1937 fairs the fairgrounds were once again used as a refugee camp for flood victims from low-lying areas in the Mississippi Valley. The flood of February 1937 was one of the worst ever in the area. This time, new makeshift structures to house the refugees were erected at the fairgrounds by the National Guard. Fairview School was used as a hospital.

By 1937 the fair was back on a good financial footing for the first time since 1929. Yet despite its best efforts, the continuation of the fair was in question. Fair officials found themselves busy explaining to the press that the fair would not be combined with the Cotton Carnival as had been suggested, and that the Park Commission's new desire to enlarge its recreation facilities at the fairgrounds could co-exist with the needs of the Mid-South Fair.

Perhaps in an effort to take advantage of new promotional techniques, 1937 fair officials worked out an arrangement with the Memphis Press Scimitar's radio station, WMPS, to broadcast live from the fair. A glass control room booth was set up, and announcers could broadcast reports on fair highlights by "remote control" from 35 different locations on the fairgrounds. Visitors to the WMPS booth were able to see as well as hear a program in progress.

It was decided that the fair would continue at the fairgrounds in 1938, but after that, the fate of the organization was once again in question. Frank Fuller, who had managed the fair since 1910, resigned that year because of ailing health. No one knew who could take his place.

*A*n outside management company from Illinois made an inquiry about taking over the management of the fair in 1939. But fair President Raymond Skinner, in late October of 1938, called a meeting with city officials and about 50 area businessmen to learn of their attitudes about the fair's management. That group voted unanimously not to consider the outside management company's proposal. Fair officials then appealed to the local businessmen to lend support by exhibiting at the fair and by helping with ticket sales. They also talked of the repairs needed at the fairgrounds because maintenance had been neglected during the deficit years of the Depression.

Even though the city still didn't renew the fair's lease on the fairgrounds, a new resolve apparently came out of that 1938 meeting to continue the fair, and to promote it to the community. Perhaps as part of the general feeling that the fair should remain a home-grown institution, the 1939 fair presented a Southern-made products exposition. Also, in an effort to draw more people, the admission price — which had gone from 75 cents in the prosperous 1920s to 50 cents during the Depression-era 1930s — was reduced to 35 cents. It was hoped that this would help make the fair accessible to more people. And it did. Attendance for the 1939 Mid-South Fair was 156,916, the highest since 1928, its last year as the Tri-State Fair. Early in 1940 the city finally renewed the fair's lease on the fairgrounds for another five years and the future of the Mid-South Fair again appeared promising.

In 1940 mechanical turnstiles were installed at the fair entrance gates to give better control over admittance, and to facilitate the tallying of money received for tickets. Better fences were also constructed around the fairgrounds to further reduce loss of money from ticket sales. However, perhaps because of the more efficient auditing techniques, 1940 saw a slump in attendance numbers. While this looked bad on paper, the new methods made the operation more professional and the fair still showed a profit that year. Fair officials, business people and the city and county governments all felt the fair had gotten past its money problems of the thirties and was ready to thrive again in the forties as it had in the twenties.

*T*he Shelby County Building was the sight of the National Dairy Show in 1941. A large arena was built in the center of the building for the show with a throne at one end to seat the lucky woman who became queen of the show. At the other end was an area set aside for the queen's court, comprised of 30 dairy cows representing five different breeds.

With that attitude in mind, fair directors voted to invite the National Dairy Show back to Memphis. The dairy industry accepted and the show was set for 1941. The fair also hosted the National Polled Hereford Show in 1941, the first time that exhibition of cattle was held in the South. On the day before the 1941 fair, Mayor Walter Chandler received a letter from President Franklin Roosevelt congratulating the Mid-South Fair and the dairy industry on their upcoming exposition.

The only problem for the 1941 fair was a bout of community objections brought on by the decision to keep the fair operating on a Sunday that year for the first time in its history. Because of the two national shows being held in conjunction with the fair, officials decided scheduling the extra day was essential to assuring success. Methodist ministers were up in arms and protested their disapproval in a letter to the Fair Association saying, "It is not a record crowd passing through the turnstiles of a fairgrounds on Sunday that brings true and enduring greatness to a city. It is righteousness and the proper regard for that which is holy that exalt a city." Fair President, Raymond Skinner replied, "Under normal conditions, I agree with the ministers and I too think that Sunday should be set aside. But this year we couldn't crowd all the events into six days." He further pointed out that the midway would not open until 1:30 on Sunday out of respect to the churches. And so it went. The 1941 fair ran for eight days from Saturday through the following Saturday. The Sunday of the fair that year set a record for second-day attendance at 36,875. Ironically, the five Methodist groups who operated food booths at the fair that Sunday made a one-day profit of more than $3,500.

Since the fair, the National Dairy Show, and the National Polled Hereford Show all did so well that year, both shows were planning to come back to Memphis in 1942. All was on the upswing for the Mid-South Fair. But once again, forces beyond fair officials' control put a damper on the momentum.

U.S. participation in World War II began in

December of 1941, and in May 1942 the Second Army asked the city to allow it to use the entire fairgrounds as a camp for the duration of the war. The city granted the request, and the 1942 Mid-South Fair was cancelled. The war lasted through 1945 and so there were no fairs again until 1947. However, the amusement park and the pool still operated under the auspices of the Park Commission during the war years.

While most of the other activity at the fairgrounds during that time was war-related, two fires which destroyed landmarks were not. In 1944 the Woman's Building was consumed by fire. And in September 1945 a fire broke out in the old grandstand and destroyed it. The Press Scimitar said of the fire, "No allied target was ever more devastated than the Fairgrounds grandstand which burned to the ground last night."

The war was over in late 1945. By the summer of 1946 the army had moved out of the fairgrounds and it was being re-tooled for the 1947 return of the Mid-South Fair. Many improvements were made and remodeling older buildings as well as rebuilding the burned structures was begun. It was proudly reported by the head of the Park Commission that the amusement park renovation would be done with the safety of the public in mind, or so he thought: "We will use concrete, brick and stone as much as possible, along with asbestos roofing, to make the amusement park as fireproof as possible."

The last three fairs of the 1940s also saw a rebuilding of the Mid-South Fair's prominence in the region. It was then being called the Mid-South Fair and Livestock Show, emphasizing its concentration on farm animals. In 1949 the old Casino was sold to the Park Commission for $15,000 by its owner Joe Bennett, who decided to retire. It was then used as a basketball court, and for some adult dances, as well as teen dances and other youth activities. Also in 1949, a "girlie show" on the midway called "Beautiful Bagdad" was ordered closed by a county commissioner. And the landmark ride Noah's Ark was torn down that year to make way for a House of Horrors.

In 1948 the eight-day exposition drew 252,209 people, and the ten-day 1949 fair drew upwards of 321,000 — more than any fair before that. Rejuvenated by all their success, fair officials were in the familiar position of once again campaigning for more space and better facilities.

The decade of the 1950s was a time of post-war prosperity for the Mid-South Fair just as it was for the nation. Fair officials were able to expand the grounds and add buildings. And finally, after 100 years of nearly consistent operation, the 1950s saw the fair find more solid and secure ground as a permanent and unquestioned annual fixture of Memphis life.

When the fairgrounds amusement park opened in May for the 1950 summer season it had been remodeled at a cost of $250,000. The most noteworthy new feature was Kiddie Land, with a miniature merry-go-round, automobiles, boats, bucking horses in a tiny corral, miniature golf, bazooka guns and basketball. New rides in the amusement park included the House of Horrors, the Caterpillar and the Curl E. Que. Another new ride called the Orbit was touted as somehow being able to move in three directions at once. Other rides had been refurbished including the Pippin, the twin Ferris Wheels, the Old Mill, the Bug, the Whip, and the Carousel.

This is all that was left of the Woman's Building after a fire there in 1944.

Mid-South Fair

1950s

A crowd entering the fairgrounds in 1952.

In time for opening day of the 1950 fair, work was completed on a new livestock arena which seated 8,000, and on a new Woman's Building to replace the old one which burned down during the war. The most talked-about exhibit that year was the Hall of Foods show put on by the Memphis Retail Grocers' Association. The show presented the processing of food from the farm to the kitchen.

In 1951 the "Progress of the American Woman" was the theme for the Women's Department. A fair official said the exhibits and demonstrations presented would "show how today's woman, through the use of labor-saving devices, has additional time off from homemaking chores to improve her self and her family in cultural development." Another exhibit that year showed the development of atomic energy and its peacetime uses.

Movies continued to be a potent force in American culture, and during the 1950s black-and-white television became a prominent part of American households as well. The stars of both mediums began to be featured at the fair. Wild Bill Elliot starred in the 1952 rodeo. The next year, the rodeo moved indoors to the Arena Building. In 1954, the Cisco Kid was featured, and Memphians also got their first taste of color television at the fair that year.

Other cultural and social trends affected the Mid-South Fair as well. In response to the emerging youth culture of the post-war baby boom, the fair created the Youth Talent Contest in 1953, which was staged at the Casino. Contestants competed in several classes of talent including vocal, instrumental, dramatic, acrobatic, dancing and novelty. The winners were picked after a series of preliminary contests throughout the region, leading to the final contests staged at the Mid-South Fair. Also in 1953, an entire building was devoted to sports, travel and vacations in response to America's growing interest in leisure activities.

One of the more intriguing incidents ever to occur on the fairgrounds was a bizarre three-alarm fire that destroyed the cattle barn in May 1955. Around 3:45 one afternoon, firemen were called to fight the huge blaze in the old wooden barn. It fed on 500 bales of hay, but luckily there were no animals in the barn. When it was over, the fire had caused $125,000 worth of damage. Arson was suspected all along and fair Manager G.W. Wynne said after the blaze, "It's been a constant problem keeping high school-age boys out of the barn."

Actually, in an unexpected twist, it turned out that the blaze was set by a group of six girls from Fairview Junior High. The girls, aged 12 to 14, had formed a gang called the "Corpas Debs" just hours before the fire. Minutes before setting the blaze, the girls drew up the by-laws of the gang which read: "1) We shall obey our leader at all times. 2) Once you get in, you can't get out. 3) If you get picked up by the cops, you must not squeal, or you will suffer the consequences. 4) You can smoke if you want to, but you do not have to." The incident was inspired by the "leader" of the group who had recently seen *Blackboard Jungle,* a movie about delinquent teenage boys. She said that although there was nothing in the movie about fire, she was influenced by it. "Those boys in the show acted big," she explained, "as if they could do everything while the girls couldn't do anything. I wanted to show that girls can do things too." After being caught at their first and only official act, all six of the Corpas Debs were

A photo from the height of the 1955 blaze set by the Corpas Debs, a gang of girls from Fairview Junior High. The fire caused $125,000 worth of damage and destroyed the cattle barn built in 1919. No animals were in the barn at the time.

convicted of the arson and sentenced to psychiatric counseling and correctional institutions. Meanwhile, fair officials got busy building a new, improved 64,000- square-foot cattle barn in time for the 1955 Mid-South Fair at a cost of $153,000.

Throughout 1956 the fair organization was hard at work planning its all-out extravaganza Centennial celebration. The Mid-South Fair promised that the Centennial would provide "history, fun and authenticity." Premiums and prizes were awarded amounting to $71,500. The centerpiece of the event was the Centennial Village, a Williamsburg-like replica of an 1856 town portraying the day-to-day existence of its people. The village contained an old barber shop, print shop, hotel, post office, tavern, general store, army recruiting station and church.

President Dwight D. Eisenhower sent a telegram to fair President Wallace Witmer congratulating the fair on its 100th year. Perhaps the climactic ceremony of the Centennial was the time capsule which fair officials buried on the fairgrounds. In it were documents depicting the present-day life in 1956, as well as the minutes from a Shelby County Agricultural Society meeting in 1856. All the information was put on microfilm and sealed in a glass bottle to be re-opened in 2056. Since atomic energy was a focus of

Fair president Wallace Witmer, and Fairest of the Fair Bobbye Harris, place the time capsule from the 1956 centennial celebration in its "tomb" at the fairgrounds to be unearthed in 2056 at the fair's bicentennial.

Western performer Lash LaRue and his sidekick Alfred St. John at the 1956 fair where they performed after being arrested.

public attention in the 1950s, someone suggested putting a radioactive substance in the neck of the bottle so that it could be located in case it was lost over the course of 100 years. It is not clear whether that was done, but possible radioactivity is worth noting for the benefit of 21st century fair officials who plan to unearth the time capsule.

The 1956 Centennial Fair had a bit of scandal, too. One of the performers, bullwhip artist and movie actor Lash LaRue, was arrested after police found in his hotel room three sewing machines and an adding machine that had been stolen from the fairgrounds. The 34-year-old Hollywood-based performer was taken into custody at the fair midway and held in city jail for five hours along with two other Hollywood-based members of his troupe, 64-year-old Alfred St. John and 20-year-old Carla Gilbert. While in jail, Gilbert apparently tried to kill herself by tying her silk scarf around her neck. When police found her, she was blue in the face and almost unconscious. An officer used a pocketknife to cut the scarf from her throat.

The three were released on a $3,500 bond that night. LaRue claimed he had bought the goods not knowing they were stolen, though the person he said sold him the stolen goods was apparently a friend of Gilbert's. Despite the scandal, LaRue's troupe went on to perform at the fair the next day and fulfilled their contract.

But of all the carefully planned and unplanned events of the 1956 Centennial celebration, the one which in retrospect might overshadow the rest is the surprise appearance of a newly famous Memphis singer named Elvis Presley. The 1956 fair opened just three weeks after Elvis' first appearance on The Ed Sullivan Show. Earlier that year he had released "Hound Dog," and "Blue Suede Shoes," and his "Heartbreak Hotel" had made it to number one on the charts.

Ironically, just a few years earlier, Elvis had competed in a preliminary round of the fair's Youth Talent Contest and had not made the cut. But by 1956 the tune had changed. No one seemed to be denying Elvis anything he wanted. It had been rumored he might make an appearance at the fair that year because singer Dennis Day was performing in the "Stars Over Dixie" revue at the Arena Building. Day was Jack Benny's right-hand man on radio and television and was also a movie actor. As part of his act he was to do an Elvis imitation which he had done many times in Las Vegas that year to the delight of Hollywood insiders. In it he impersonated a Japanese singer wearing blue suede shoes and imitating Elvis.

Sure enough, on the evening of Day's performance, Elvis drove up to the fair on his Harley-Davidson motorcycle with up-and-coming Hollywood teen idol Nick Adams on board. The two toured the fairgrounds and then caught the "Stars Over Dixie" show. After Day's imitation, Elvis came to the stage, praised the parody and kidded with Day. The Commercial Appeal reported how he also joked about $5,500 he had just lost in a settlement to a young Memphis woman:

> *Ambling to the microphone the rock and roll king asked, "Is there anybody here I can lay my head on their shoulder and have my picture taken?"*
>
> *The star was referring to his out-of-court settlement with Miss Robbie Moore of 431 Stonewall, who threatened legal action after Elvis published a picture that showed his head on her shoulder. The photo appeared in Presley's fan magazine, Elvis Presley Speaks.*

The previous attendance record of 360,354 was broken by this seven-year-old girl at the 1956 fair Centennial. She and her mother won two tickets to see the "Stars Over Dixie" feature performance at the fair that year. A surprise guest performer at that show was a local boy named Elvis Presley.

That was the last time Elvis made a public appearance at the fair. He did, however, rent out the fairgrounds amusement park many times from then on for his famous late-night private parties. Although no one knew at the time how the magnitude of his fame would increase, Elvis was probably the biggest-name entertainer who ever appeared at the fair. Still, from 1956 on, big-name attractions became more and more common, and even expected.

By the late 1950s the fair was thriving. The Lone Ranger and Tonto appeared at the 1957 fair. Local WHBQ radio deejay George Klein started Teen Town in 1957 where kids danced to the latest music of the day. Advertisements for Teen Town said, "It's HEPSVILLE like … A swinging record hop that's really way out … with WHBQ deejays making with cool sounds … you know … like WOW!"

In 1958 a new site for the Mid-South Fair was frequently discussed. Places suggested ranged from Riverside Park to the Penal Farm to a tract of land near the airport. Ultimately, the fair stayed put. In 1959 there was talk of building a huge football stadium and a coliseum to seat 20,000 year-round. It was the appearance of Roy Rogers and Dale Evans at the fair in 1959 that was used as prime evidence in the campaign for building the coliseum, because the western stars sold out the 8,000-seat Arena Building and people had to be turned away.

With the arrival of the 1960s, during the terms of fair presidents Boyd Arthur and Walter Dilatush, a new era of prosperity seemed to be dawning for the Mid-South Fair. The organization stood ready to make full use of the fairgrounds by building a coliseum and football stadium, and by reorganizing other parts of the site. To get this job underway, fair officials pinned their hopes on the advice of someone who knew a lot about fairs — Art Linkletter.

The Roy Rogers and Dale Evans show at the fairgrounds Arena Building in 1959 drew the largest crowd (8,000) for a single event in the fair's previous history. Many people couldn't see and others had to be turned away. In this picture, Roy takes his horse Trigger through a series of tricks. The attendance at this performance was used as "colossal proof" of the need to build a coliseum.

Dale Evans and Roy Rogers congratulated a 4-year-old girl for being the one-half millionth visitor to the fair in 1959. The Roy Rogers and Dale Evans show was credited with putting the fair over that half-million attendance mark for the first time in its history.

THE 1959 FAIR BROKE PREVIOUS ATTENDANCE RECORDS BY ATTRACTING MORE THAN A HALF-MILLION VISITORS. FULL OF THE OPTIMISM THAT A SERIES OF SUCCESSFUL FAIRS HAD FOSTERED, THE MID-SOUTH FAIR APPROACHED THE 1960S WITH THE IDEA OF DEVELOPING THE CURRENT SITE INTO A MULTI-MILLION-DOLLAR "DREAM" FAIRGROUNDS OVER THE NEXT DECADE.

Mid-South Fair

1960s & 1970s

A drawing of the proposal that Art Linkletter's company presented to fair officials for revamping the fairgrounds in 1960. Note the lake with fountains and boats that run down the middle of the picture. This plan was never realized.

At that time the celebrity entertainer, famous for his television shows with kids, worked with a partner, Clyde Vandeburg. Together they were consultants to fairs nationwide, and they advised the Mid-South Fair on renovation of its fairgrounds. The partners presented a 100-page, ten-year plan to fair and city officials in June 1960 to then President Boyd Arthur. The plan called for building the Mid-South Coliseum on its present site. But almost nothing else in the plan was implemented. An example of one idea that didn't pan out was: a proposed 700-foot-long lagoon between the Shelby County Building and East Parkway usable for motor boat shows and other water shows. The Linkletter plan also proposed a new Woman's Building to be constructed over the swimming pool that would incorporate the pool and be "one of the most unique facilities of its kind in the country."

The Linkletter plan did, however, serve to motivate the city to act on development of the fairgrounds. By 1963, under fair President Weldon Burrow, ground was broken for the new coliseum. The old Casino and agriculture buildings were both condemned by the city, and demolished in 1963. The new coliseum was dedicated in 1964. That same year Joe Pipkin was elected president of the fair and served as chairman for 15 years, fair president for 5 years, and coliseum chairman for 17 years. The Liberty Bowl Memorial Stadium opened in September of the following year.

The sixties also saw the addition of a minor-league baseball stadium. Then called Blues Stadium, it became the home of the The Memphis Blues baseball team. The team is now called the Memphis Chickasaws and the ball park was re-named Tim

McCarver Stadium. To round out the decade, a new athletic building and exhibition hall were added in 1965. And in 1968 the Mid-South Fair office building was constructed and the fair management offices moved from their long-time home in the old Horticulture Building.

Another notable building became a functioning part of the fair in the 1960s. It was an old Quonset hut which had been moved to the fairgrounds in 1959 from Poplar Avenue and Union Extended where, in the late 1930s, it had once housed Memphis grocery store magnate Clarence Saunder's "Keedoozle," a failed concept for a key-operated, automated grocery store. In 1960, just after its arrival at the fairgrounds, the Quonset hut became the home of the Park Commission's Memphis Children's Theatre. Started by Lucile Ewing in 1940, the year-round theatre served generations of Memphis kids from all parts of the city as a creative outlet run by children and for children. It stayed in its fairgrounds location until the early 1980s, when the organization moved to another location and left the Quonset hut behind.

But physical changes weren't the only progressions the fair made in the 1960s. In 1962 the Mid-South Fair once again became a racially integrated event. Blacks and whites of the Mid-South could now enjoy and participate in the fair together, and the contributions of all races would slowly become integral parts of the Mid-South Fair.

Through all the development and progress, entertainment was turning into an even more prominent aspect of the fair. In 1960, Ricky Nelson, a "heart throb of young America" performed at the fair. He had launched a singing career on his parents' television show, The Adventures of Ozzie and Harriet a few years before, and young Memphis was thrilled at his appearance. In 1961, "Baker," a monkey who was "America's first astronaut" appeared. Andy Griffith was the headliner in 1962. All of the original Beverly Hillbillies except Uncle Jed were featured for two days at the

This billboard announced that the Beverly Hillbillies would be the featured stars of the 1963 rodeo.

rodeo in 1963. And the Three Stooges were the first day's rodeo entertainment that same year. In 1964, Lorne Greene and Dan Blocker — Ben and Hoss Cartwright of the TV show, Bonanza — took part in the World Championship Rodeo. The Cartwrights came back to the fair throughout the sixties and Michael Landon (Little Joe Cartwright) joined them.

In 1966 the rodeo was held in the new Coliseum for the first time. In 1967, Jim Nabors, who was TV's "Gomer Pyle" appeared at the rodeo, along with a return performance by Roy Rogers and Dale Evans. Johnny Cash was the headliner at the coliseum in 1968, and Tammy Wynette and Charley Pride performed there the next year. The Memphis State-Ole Miss football game was held at the new football stadium in 1968 during the fair.

Free features at the fair in the 1960s included the very popular Eldon Roark's Museum of Unnatural History which started in 1961, and moved into the coliseum in 1965. Each year the Memphis Press-Scimitar columnist brought together "quaint oddities, rare curiosities and whatzits" and put them on display for all to see. For years, the museum was one of the fair's most popular attractions.

An antique auto show in 1961 featured a Model T race. A duck-calling contest was added in 1962. In 1966, the Children's Barnyard featured a baby chick midway with 150 baby chicks wandering about on a 40-foot table amid tiny replicas of midway attractions on which the chicks rode. Feed bowls on the miniature rides induced them aboard.

In 1963 a trend of mischief developed at the Old Mill ride. In October, three boys were caught pouring detergent into the circulating water that propelled the boats through the tunnel of the ride. The boys said they did it "to see what would happen." Workmen had to cut off the ride, drain the canals and clean them. This was the fifth time that season that soap or detergent had been poured into the water and the second time an arrest was made.

The contests and agricultural aspects of the fair continued to be important features, but were beginning to be rivaled in scope by the big-name entertainment. Attendance in 1968 was reported to be more than 700,000. Such growth was attributed to the headline entertainment and the ability of the new facilities to handle that many people. However, there is some question as to how accurate the attendance figures for the fair were during this period since counting

*P*lacards and signs advertised the fair's most popular attractions in the mid-1960s.

methods were not as scientific as they became in the mid-seventies. Therefore, those attendance figures are generally considered to be broad estimates.

During the late sixties, the social revolution that was taking place in America surprisingly had very little effect on the fair. The biggest changes of that time were comparatively minor. In 1967 the beauty contest title of "Fairest of the Fair" was changed to "Miss Mid-South Fair" so that the queen could be chosen before the fair and be available for advance promotional activities. In 1966 the Miss Youth Personality Contest, for young women from 14 to 17 years old, was added to the Miss Mid-South Fair Contest. Miss Youth Personality in 1968 was future Board President Debbie Branan. A cheerleading contest began in 1967 as well. Meanwhile, the Woman's Department changed its name to The Family Living Center and by 1969 the Eldon Roark Museum had run its course and was cancelled.

*P*ranksters dumped detergent into the waters that propelled these log boats through the Old Mill ride in 1963. It happened seven times in one summer, but only twice were kids caught in the act and taken to Juvenile Court.

By the 1970s, a popular idea was the development of a year-round theme park on the fairgrounds amusement park site. In 1970, under fair President John Ellis, a proposal for Libertyland, financed by the Mid-South Fair, was being drawn up behind the scenes. Meanwhile, Ed Sullivan taped a $250,000 segment for his Sunday night CBS broadcast at Blues Stadium during the 1970 Mid-South Fair. Jerry Lee Lewis, Loretta Lynn and Bob Hope performed for the crowds, and a new moonrock, brought back to earth by the first moon-walking astronauts in 1969, was on display under tight security.

In 1971 the Libertyland proposal was approved by the city and county and its details were worked out. While President Lee Winchester was at the helm of the fair, improvements in the roads at the fairgrounds were made and air-conditioning was added to most fair buildings. Sadly, another case of arson plagued the fairgrounds that year. This time the culprits were a gang of boys who left behind hand-painted cryptic symbols at the sites of their destruction. Before they were caught, $100,000 in damage had been done in seven fires at the fairgrounds and in the surrounding area.

The 1971 entertainment bill included legendary country stars. Johnny Cash and his wife June Carter performed, along with her famous mother, Maybelle Carter, and the renowned Carter Family. Carl Perkins and the Statler Brothers were also on the bill. In addition, Roy Clark and teen idol Bobby Sherman performed.

The 1971 fair introduced a new type of agricultural exhibition, as the fair hosted its first tractor pull contest in the Arena Building. There was also a circus, a petting zoo and of course, the World Championship Rodeo which included bareback riding, brahma bull riding, calf roping and a girls' barrel race.

Sonny & Cher performed for 1972 fair audiences, and over the next few years, big-name performers included Mac Davis, Charley Pride, Dolly Parton, Crystal Gayle and others. In an attempt to reach a broader audience, the fair hosted a concert by the soul group the Ohio Players in 1977. Among other hits, the Ohio Players were famous for a song called "Love Roller Coaster."

Although entertainment continued to be a big draw for the city folk of Memphis, the farming and rural communities of the region were still omnipresent at the fair. By 1972 livestock from 20 states was being exhibited. The premiums for that fair amounted to more than $80,000. In 1973, large 2,000- to 4,000-pound cattle were on display.

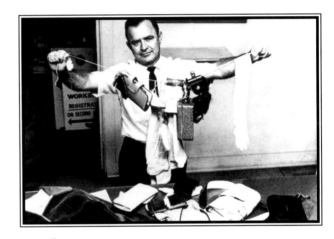

A fair official showed just a few of the more than 100 items in the lost and found pile at the 1968 Mid-South Fair.

This billboard outside the fairgrounds advertised a historic country music show at the Mid-South Fair in 1971.

Odd exhibits and features still popped up during the fairs of the 1970s. In 1973, with William H. Austin as the president of the fair, there was a timely display of something called a "Watergate Quilt." In 1972 there was a computer-generated talking Abe Lincoln. An old log cabin from the late 1700s was found in Bethesda, Tennessee, in the early 1970s and moved to the fairgrounds for display. It was carefully restored and furnished with pieces from the early pioneer period. In 1976 a midway side show featured, "The Ugliest Man In The World." The next year, Roman gladiator wrestling took place at the coliseum featuring the well-known local wrestler Jerry Lawler.

In 1977 during the term of fair President Jack H. Morris, III, a serious proposal was made to put a plastic dome over the entire fairgrounds. Models were designed, plans were circulated, but somewhere along the way the idea faded. However, from the late-sixties through the mid-seventies, other capital improvements did occur at the fairgrounds. The Pipkin Center exhibit building and the Youth Center exhibit building were constructed, and the Woman's Building was renovated with the city, the county and the Mid-South Fair jointly contributing to the costs. The Shelby County Building was completely renovated during this time and trailer park facilities were also added to the fairgrounds to accommodate exhibitors and entertainers. These new and renovated buildings were put to more use year-round as were the entire fairgrounds. It became an entertainment and sporting event center for Memphis. Also, a flea market was held there on weekends which still runs to the present day.

On July 4, 1976, the day of America's 200th anniversary, Libertyland theme park opened at the fairgrounds. It hosted a unique and fitting observance of the Bicentennial. Everything was red, white and blue that day, and through three themed areas visitors viewed American history — Colonial Land, Turn of the Century Land, and Frontier Land. There was also an authentic replica of the Liberty Bell on the grounds. In order to accommodate Libertyland, all of the rides in the old amusement park were torn down except the Pippin and the Grand Carousel. The

These two teens compared report cards at the 1973 fair. For every "A" they got two free rides, for every "B" they got one free ride.

The James Waddy log cabin, dated back to the late 1700s, was bought by the Mid-South Fair, dismantled, transported from Middle Tennessee, and re-assembled at the fairgrounds in the 1970s.

Pippin was re-named the "Zippin Pippin" and the area was totally re-landscaped. Incidentally, the Grand Carousel was moved 92 feet northeast to a new location.

When Libertyland opened in 1976, with Tom O'Brien as president, the way the Mid-South Fair was run changed. Although the two ventures were separate, they were under the same roof, and Libertyland management was made part of the fair staff. The Libertyland Committee was made up

The Pippin was the only ride besides the Grand Carousel that was left standing when the fairgrounds amusement park was dismantled in the mid-1970s to make way for Libertyland theme park.

Mayor Wyeth Chandler, Shelby County Mayor Roy Nixon, Jack Morris III, Olin Morris, Joe Pipkin, Dan Wilkinson and Lee Winchester. As that reorganization of management fell into place, both Libertyland and the fair continued to develop through the 1970s. This was especially reflected in the variety of contests at the Mid-South Fair. The fair permanently became a ten-day event in 1978, a change initiated by President James W. Campbell, Jr. It sponsored youth contests, agricultural contests, cheerleading contests, beauty contests, talent contests, culinary contests, senior citizen contests, baby contests and others.

The opening of Libertyland meant 300 new jobs were created. And ever since then, the theme park has continued to provide 300-400 jobs for the community, especially for teenagers, during the summer. Many of the performers who got their start at Libertyland have gone on to careers in professional entertainment.

In 1979 the fair broke all previous accurate attendance records with a crowd of 466,845. The increase was attributed in part to the two sold-out coliseum shows on Saturday, September 29, by Kenny Rogers and Dottie West which grossed more than $190,000, and a Memphis State vs. Texas A&M football game in Liberty Bowl Memorial Stadium. That busy Saturday produced a one-day high in gate, ride and food operation revenues.

With these successes, the fair organization entered the 1980s on the road to having the most diversified mix of rural and urban attractions ever in its history and with the interest and participation from the community at a high point.

Mid-South   Fair

1 9 8 0 s   a n d   1 9 9 0 s

The presidential election of 1980 between then-President Jimmy Carter and his challenger Ronald Reagan came to Memphis. Vice President Walter Mondale officially opened the 1980 Mid-South Fair. Of course, Mondale made a speech. In it he stressed his stance as a "friend of the farmer" by extolling the virtues of the family-owned farm. He also went to the Children's Barnyard and posed for pictures with a donkey, the symbol of his Democratic Party. Mondale is the highest-ranking U.S. government official ever to visit the Mid-South Fair.

The fair had intended that year to experiment with a different kind of concert, pairing famous bandleader Doc Severinsen with the Memphis Symphony Orchestra at the coliseum. But plans to serve champagne at the event violated state liquor laws, and Severinsen and company felt the champagne was an important element of the event. By mutual agreement between Severinsen and the Mid-South Fair management, the concert was cancelled just days before the fair opening. This was the first time a coliseum event had ever been cancelled. Still, Loretta Lynn, Eddie Rabbit, Lynn Anderson and the Bar-Kays all performed that year.

The Mid-South Fair celebrated its own achievements in 1981, marking its 125th anniversary. In a special commemorative program, fair President William W. Farris echoed the theme upon which the fair had been built when he said, "This is a time for Memphis and the Mid-South to celebrate the heritage of our past and the promise of our future. ... As the Mid-South strives to combine industry and agriculture, so the Mid-South Fair interweaves the best of modern entertainment with exhibits of the fruits of agriculture."

By 1981, the 28-year-old Youth Talent Contest had grown to great proportions thanks to WREG-TV and the Memphis Press-Scimitar. More than 15,000 people, ages 10-21, competed that year, making it the largest amateur youth talent contest in the world. That year fair officials built upon the local competition. Incoming President Olin Morris added an additional international event in which the top prize was $7,500 in cash and merchandise. The 1981 grand prize winner of both the Mid-South and the first international contest was a Memphis dancer named Eric Henderson. He went on to co-star in two Janet Jackson videos and still works as a dancer in Hollywood. The next year's winner of the Mid-South Youth Talent Contest also went on to national success. She was a Memphis entertainer named Wendy Moten who has a successful career as a rhythm-and-blues singer.

The Dallas Cowboy Cheerleaders appeared at the 125th anniversary fair. And Elvis was sighted at the fair that year — an Elvis sculpted in butter, that is. One exhibitor put a new twist on the old tradition of butter sculptures depicting dairy scenes and cows which were first displayed at fairs in the 1930s. Celebrating the heroes of the times, the 1980s butter sculptures were of celebrities. Elvis was the first, and in 1982, Dolly Parton was the subject. Michael Jackson was immortalized in 1984, complete with his famous glove.

Throughout the eighties, the fair continued to attract a variety of big-name entertainers. Under President Dan Wilkinson, Willie Nelson and George Strait appeared in 1984 and the then up-and-coming mother/daughter group, the Judds (Wynonna and her mother Naomi), performed in 1985. There was a controversy in 1985 when the heavy-metal band Motley Crüe was scheduled to play at the coliseum during the fair. To the dismay of many rockers, Wilkinson ended up cancelling the show, saying it was "not family entertainment."

The next year, the immensely popular British rock star Elton John played the fair, as well as the Miami Sound Machine. In 1987 The Temptations and Marie Osmond appeared. Jerry Lee Lewis was also scheduled to play that year but cancelled the show because President Chuck Pierotti was served an IRS tax levy saying if Lewis played they would take the proceeds from the show to settle Lewis' IRS debt.

Obviously, many performers liked coming to the Mid-South Fair as much as fair-goers liked seeing them. The fair has had many entertainers who return to the crowds in successive years. For instance, in 1988, President Oscar Edmonds contracted the Miami Sound Machine to come back and headline with Conway Twitty, Loretta Lynn and Ray Charles. And in 1989, the Oak Ridge Boys, Kool & the Gang, Three Dog Night and Tanya Tucker performed.

Free entertainment and attractions continued to vary in the 1980s. In 1982 the World Pro Armwrestling Championships were held at the Mid-South Fair for the first time. More than 300 competitors from 45 states participated. Also that year one of the entrants in the art displays was Tennessee Senator Howard Baker. His respected photos were well-received. Pig

races started at the fair in 1985. Pigs chased Oreo cookies around a 150-foot track. A frog hypnotist came to the fair in 1987. After he put his frogs in trances they proceeded to lift weights, imitate celebrities and ride bikes. In 1989 there was a twins' contest at the fair. Throughout the 1980s, local television newscasts were broadcast from the fair all week.

By 1984, premiums for the fair were up to $115,000 and admission was $3.75. The next year the idea of possibly moving the fair was again debated. A master plan was drawn up to relocate to a site at the Agricenter in East Memphis. It would cover 275 acres and include 119 acres of parking and an amphitheater seating 15,000. The cost of relocation was estimated at $14 million at the time. That plan was never realized. There was also talk that year of building a new sports arena at the fairgrounds, but the idea was scrapped and the new arena, The Pyramid, was built downtown instead.

The beginning of the 1990s was the first time in fair history that a woman became the president of the Mid-South Fair. Debra Pace Branan, who had been the 1968 Miss Youth Personality, took over the reins of leadership in 1990. For the two years she was president the fair broke all previous attendance records. In 1990 there were 492,975 fairgoers, outpacing the old record of 466,845 from 1979. Then in

Painters made signs promoting the 1981 Mid-South Fair.

1991 that record was eclipsed when fair attendance reached 565,615.

During those two years the entertainers performing at the fair included The Judds, Charlie Daniels, Conway Twitty and Ricky Skaggs in 1990; and Amy Grant, Vince Gill, Travis Tritt, Garth Brooks and Patti Labelle in 1991. By 1992, the fair was again attracting a diversity of entertainers including George Jones, Willie Nelson and the young rap duo Kris Kross.

In 1991 and 1992, during the terms of Presidents Robert Bowers and Debra Pace Branan, represented by Oscar Edmonds, the city and county governments settled the remainder of the $13.2 million in principal and interest owed on bond issues from the 1970s for construction of Libertyland. The Mid-South Fair had repaid $6.2 million of the original $9.8 million borrowed from the city and county up to that point. While the fair had been profitable in the years prior, Libertyland profits never covered its original construction costs and the fair had to pay the difference. The settlement was made when it was determined that Libertyland would never generate the revenues originally projected by Economic Research Associates of Los Angeles and that Libertyland would continue to drain the proceeds generated by the Mid-South Fair.

One more threat to the fair's location came in 1993 while Robert Bowers was president. Memphis bid to procure one of the National Football League's two expansion teams. If Memphis had won a team, it would have been called the Hound Dogs. This would have meant an expansion of Liberty Bowl Memorial Stadium and a possible relocation for the fair. However, the teams were eventually awarded to other cities and the fair once again stayed put.

By 1993, the total premiums for the Mid-South Fair amounted to $263,661, with livestock premiums making up the bulk of that at $225,654. Thus, the fair remained true to its original agricultural heritage, even while it continued to grow and diversify through the 1980s and 1990s. Now, as it poises itself to enter the 21st century, the Mid-South Fair is the city's most enduring annual event. In 1993, the Mid-South Fair drew people from 24 states and all walks of life to the historic 176-acre fairgrounds in the center of the city. It did so with the same tried-and-true mix of excitement, enlightenment, relevance, and plain old fun that has been bringing out the autumn crowds continually since that first fair in 1856 drew so many Memphians to that long-lost, serene grove near Mr. Brinkley's place, just outside of the city.

C H A P T E R
Four

Livestock Contests

*A*N OWNER SHOWS OFF HIS TWO-YEAR-OLD
GRAND CHAMPION HEREFORD BULL AT THE
MID-SOUTH FAIR IN 1947.

*M*iss Arkansas Pork Queen of 1972, Vikki McFarlin, admires Kent Clipman's blue ribbon pig. It matches her sparkling crown which is also in the shape of a pig.

*I*n the early morning a 15-year-old boy sweeps up his swine pen at the 1983 Mid-South Fair.

This polled Hereford is washed in preparation for competition at the 1953 Mid-South Fair.

In 1977, farmer Jimmy Hester spends the night in the pen to keep a watchful eye on his prize-winning pigs. This is normal practice for farmers of livestock contest contenders at the fair.

*V*ictor Domino, another polled Hereford, has her hair blown dry to make the cow ready for the show ring at the 1975 Mid-South Fair.

A little girl milks this cow at the 1977 Mid-South Fair.

A livestock parade at the 1916 fair.

Livestock and their keepers wait to be judged at the 1916 fair.

Pigs are judged in the ring as spectators look on.

Cattle are judged in 1960.

Culinary Contests

$\mathscr{A}$t the 1949 fair Mrs. Asbury Jones won a blue ribbon for this cake with the same recipe her mother had used to win a blue ribbon 13 years earlier in the same Mid-South Fair cake baking contest.

Judges take a close look at one of the baking entries.

In 1976, 15-year-old Joey Gionti became the first male best-of-show award winner with his rum pound cake in the fair's cake baking contest.

*C*anning award winners are grouped by class in this classic photograph of a traditional fair competition.

This man gets a hot mouthful at a chili pepper-eating contest.

*T*he best chili is yet to be selected as judges taste the entries in the chili contest.

Needlework • Horticulture • Baby Picture Contests

𝒯HESE WOMEN DISPLAY THEIR PRIZE-WINNING

NEEDLEWORK AT THE 1975 MID-SOUTH FAIR.

*K*irk Keiser was all smiles after becoming the Grand Prize winner of the Baby Picture Contest in 1972.

*F*lower judging in progress at the woman's building.

Beauty Contests

By 1968 the name of the beauty pageant had been changed

from Fairest of the Fair to Miss Mid-South Fair. These entrants

from East Memphis stood in front of the sign for the new fair

office building. Contestants ranged in age from 18 to 25.

In a photo that was obviously more light-hearted in its time than it would be today, the 1969 Miss Mid-South Fair, Joy Wimberley, shows a Treasury Department agent how to operate a sub-machine gun at the government agency's fair exhibit booth.

Laddie, the world's largest horse in 1970, weighing in at 3,200 pounds, caught the attention of Miss Mid-South Fair, Linda Thompson and Princess Soroya the year's National Soybean Queen. Laddie came to the fair from Clydes, Scotland.

Debbie Salter, the first alternate in the 1969 Miss Mid-South Fair Pageant, tries to coax a smile out of Yogi, a Hereford bull from Indiana.

*S*ixty-three-year-old George Eckert receives a congratulatory kiss from one Mid-South Fair pageant winner to another in 1978. The senior contests were added in the 1970s.

*C*ontestants line up in the Fairest of the Fair contest in 1956.

Youth Talent Contests

*M*EMPHIS SINGER WENDY MOTEN WON THE YOUTH TALENT CONTEST IN 1982. SHE WENT ON TO BECOME A WELL-KNOWN NATIONAL RECORDING ARTIST WITH HER RHYTHM AND BLUES HITS.

*N*ative Memphis dancer Eric Henderson won both the regional Youth Talent Contest and the first International Youth Talent Contest in 1981. He also danced at Libertyland. Henderson went on to become a successful professional dancer whose work in television, film, stage and video includes co-starring with Janet Jackson in her hit music video "When I Think of You."

Cheerleading & Baton Twirling Contests

CHEERLEADING IS SERIOUS BUSINESS AT THE

MID-SOUTH FAIR'S CHEERLEADING CONTEST.

HERE CHEERLEADERS COMPETE IN THE 1980S.

IN 1955, THE BATON TWIRLING

CONTEST WAS ALSO A BIG PART OF THE

MID-SOUTH FAIR. THESE FIVE YOUNG

LADIES ALL HAD HOPES OF WINNING

THE CONTEST.

Auto Racing

𝒯HE NEWEST KIND OF RACES WERE A BIG ATTRAC-

TION AND WERE ADVERTISED IN THE STREETS OF

MEMPHIS DURING THE YEARS OF THE TRI-STATE FAIR.

*T*he Grandstand during an auto race at the 1939 fair.

*D*aredevil auto racers were called Hell Drivers in the 1930s. Here is Hell Driver "Lucky Teeter" at the fair.

Exhibits

OMEN OF THE MEMORIAL CIRCLE OF KING'S DAUGHTERS

ORGANIZATION SOLD KARO KISSES CANDY FOR FIVE CENTS

AT THE TRI-STATE FAIR IN 1918.

This Cracker Jacks booth attracted hungry and well-dressed crowds at the 1917 Tri-State Fair.

The United States Army set up an exhibit at the Tri-State Fair in 1918 to recruit soldiers for World War I.

The Navy and Marine branches of the military also set up an exhibit at the 1918 Tri-State Fair for recruiting.

In 1933 the Schmidt School of Taxidermy had an exhibit at the Mid-South Fair.

The Dixie Motor Sales Company exhibit displayed a touring car and a roadster in 1918. The cars featured electric lights and a new air-cooled engine.

A chicken was given the "once over" and then some at the Tri-State Fair in 1917.

A poultry exhibit at the 1931 Mid-South Fair warns about some of the hazards of chicken raising, such as: rain, overheating, overcrowding, rats and bad feed, among others.

A̶t the 1931 fair cold bottles of a new drink called Orange Crush were available for sampling.

A̶ woman played peek-a-boo around the shower curtain of the J.W. Hull Plumbing and Heating bathroom exhibit in 1917.

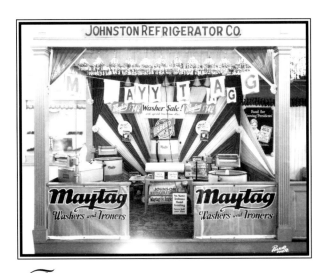

The Johnston Refrigerator company exhibited Maytag products in 1933 when the newest washing machines sold for $74.50.

The D. Canale & Company exhibit at the 1934 fair featured a seven-man band making what must have been very distinctive music in front of the company's food crates and apple baskets. The ensemble included guitars, a mandolin, a violin, a harmonica, a three-string bass played with a leather glove, and a self-made instrument in the center comprised of skillets.

*Chinchillas were raised for their fur and displayed at
the Mid-South Fair in the 1950s.*

*Press-Scimitar newspaper columnist Eldon
Roark's Museum of Unnatural History displayed strange, curious, and funny things
which attracted hordes of fair visitors in the
1960s. Here a couple enjoys this "egg plant" at
Roark's museum in 1962.*

*E*ldon Roark and Mayor Henry Loeb pose in front of the free wishing well in Roark's museum in 1961. No coins were necessary when Mayor Loeb reportedly used his one wish to ask for a balanced city budget with no tax increases.

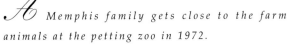
A Memphis family gets close to the farm animals at the petting zoo in 1972.

*P*lanned Parenthood workers make their educational exhibit ready for the 1978 Mid-South Fair.

WOMEN DEMONSTRATE QUILT-MAKING AT

THE FAMILY LIVING CENTER DURING THE

1977 MID-SOUTH FAIR.

The difference in clothing styles over the years are clear in this shot of a 1972 woman viewing an outfit from many years earlier at a clothing exhibit at that year's fair.

New trends in men's fashion were on parade at an evening show during the 1971 fair. All of these models were fair officials. From Left to right: (A) Joe Davis, Jr., Wayne Grout, Ray Strong, R. William Skinner.

ormer Memphis Mayor E. H. Crump's 1938 Cadillac was among the autos on display at an auto show during the 1977 fair. The owners, pictured here, lent the car Mayor Crump used to be chauffeured around town, to the exhibit.

*E*ducating the public about health was the purpose of some fair exhibits.

*I*n 1960 this display showed the various ways to be prepared for nuclear attack.

The benefits of milk are exalted by this display.

*Canning display by
4-H girls in 1938.*

C H A P T E R
Six

Celebrities and Entertainment

Politicians

*M*emphis' political boss E. H. Crump visited the Mid-South Fair in the 1940s with his family.

*M*ayor Crump and family in front of the Old Mill ride in the 1940s.

Vice President Walter Mondale officially opened the Mid-South Fair in 1980. His three-hour stopover in Memphis during the 1980 presidential election included some campaigning.

Mayor Henry Loeb, Fairest of the Fair Elizabeth Griffith and County Commission Chairman Jack Ramsay cut the ribbon to officially open the 1962 Mid-South Fair.

Tennessee Governor Buford Ellington greeted fair visitors in 1967 and officially opened the nine-day run of the Mid-South Fair.

Entertainers

WESTERN ACTOR WILD BILL ELLIOTT AND HIS HORSE POSE IN THE RODEO ARENA BEFORE HIS APPEARANCE AT THE MID-SOUTH FAIR IN THE EARLY 1950S.

*W*ild Bill Elliott thrilled kids who mimicked his gun-toting pose during the Mid-South Fair in the early 1950s.

*F*amous cowboy Cisco Kid signed autographs and posed with kids at the fair in the early 1950s.

This promotional picture ran in the Press-Scimitar after television stars the Lone Ranger and Tonto agreed to appear at the Mid-South Fair rodeo in 1957. The pair showed quick-draw skill and rope tricks and gave away silver bullets. They were so popular at the time that they appeared again for six shows at the fairgrounds amusement park a few years later in 1963.

Roy Rogers' famous horse, Trigger, bowed as a greeting to all the boys and girls of Memphis before his appearance at the 1954 fair. He is pictured here with trainer Glenn Randall.

Roy Rogers and Dale Evans replace the tie of Earl Moreland, manager of WMCT, as the broadcast company was called then, with a Mid-South Fair tie, so he could help them encourage Memphians to attend their performances in 1959.

Dale Evans, a former Memphian, and Roy Rogers came back to Memphis to perform again at the Mid-South Coliseum during the 1967 Mid-South Fair.

Fair officials signed up Roy Rogers and Dale Evans for the Mid-South Fair in 1959. Here Dale holds a card showing the dates she and her husband and their western-musical revue appeared in the Arena Building at the fair.

*C*ast members of the original "Beverly Hillbillies," Irene Ryan (Granny), Max Baer, Jr. (Jethro), and Donna Douglas (Elly May), met with fair officials in Lexington, Kentucky, before their appearance at the Mid-South Fair in 1963.

*A*ll of the cast from "The Beverly Hillbillies" except Buddy Ebson (Uncle Jed) performed at the 1963 fair. Here they cuddled up to a Memphis icon King Cotton, made from bales of cotton, in the lobby of the Peabody Hotel.

*M*emphis' own funny vampire, Sivad, host of the popular 1960s local TV show "Fantastic Features" attracted an overflow crowd of 30,000 young fans to the fairgrounds amusement park in 1963. Sivad was actually a local ad man named W. Watson Davis. The name "Sivad" is "Davis" spelled backwards.

*T*he Three Stooges also appeared at the fair in 1963. Here they pose with then-Miss Tennessee Martha Ellen Truett.

*T*he Cartwrights from the TV show "Bonanza," Dan Blocker (Hoss) and Lorne Greene (Ben), sign their names on the dotted line of a contract for seven appearances at the Mid-South Fair in 1964.

*E*d Sullivan taped a part of his popular Sunday-night television show at Blues Baseball Stadium (now Tim McCarver Stadium) during the Mid-South Fair in 1970.

*J*OHNNY CASH ATE A PRONTO PUP ON THE

MIDWAY WITH HIS WIFE JUNE CARTER CASH

AT THE MID-SOUTH FAIR IN 1968.

Garth Brooks shared a moment backstage with fair president Debra Pace Branan in 1991.

Cher was well-protected at the Mid-South Fair in 1972.

Betty White met visitors at the 1957 fair.

*B*utter sculptures were all the rage at the Mid-
South Fair in the early 1980s; both Dolly Parton
and Michael Jackson were subjects.

Midway • Free Entertainment

$\mathscr{L}$ITTLE KEWPIE DOLLS ARE LINED UP AND WAITING

TO BE WON BY FAIR-GOERS WILLING TO PLAY AN EARLY

GAME OF CHANCE AT THE 1917 TRI-STATE FAIR.

*W*earing a big, foam cowboy hat was one way to make a fashion statement at the 1980 Mid-South Fair.

*T*he options are many for this nine-year-old when choosing the right prize after winning a midway game at the fair in 1976.

*T*his woman won a handful of stuffed animals and other prizes from the midway at the 1972 fair.

*N*ot even those plaid pants could hide this woman's true weight from the expert guesser on the midway in 1974.

A midway worker calls out to fair-goers beckoning them to play a game of poker on the midway in 1976.

The fortune-telling hen gave this 15-year-old a glimpse of her future for 25 cents. When a customer put a quarter in the slot Little Gypsy Hen bent forward and pulled a ring to discharge a fortune card.

Balloons are fun for all kids, and this little girl reached for a jumbo, bouncy, ball-like one at the 1972 fair.

Large crowds filled the midway at the 1966 fair.

Donkey rides were also popular with kids at the 1973 fair.

*Sabu, one of the elephants on display at the 1967 fair
takes this three-year-old for a ride.*

*I*N THE EARLY 1950S, A CHILD,

DRESSED IN FULL WESTERN GEAR,

RIDES A HORSE AT LEAST THREE

TIMES HIS HEIGHT AROUND THE

FAIRGROUNDS AS THE FAIR'S RODEO

IS ADVERTISED BEHIND HIM.

This diving mule had a monkey on his back at the fair in the early 1980s.

An organ grinder and his monkey entertained adults and children at the 1971 Mid-South Fair.

*A*nother special day was Camera Day on which anyone with a camera got in free
until 5:00 p.m. Here press photographers pose with Miss Mid-South in 1969.

*O*ne of the fair's special days was
Handicapped Person's Day in 1973
when the fair was free for anyone
who was disabled.

*S*enior Americans Day at the fair in 1975
brought out two women who show they're actually kids at heart as they carry balloons along
the fair's midway.

Jimmie Lynch and his death dodgers smashed and crashed automobiles at high speeds to thrill fair-goers in 1941.

Truck and tractor pulls became very popular attractions in the 1980s.

Rides • Amusement Park

𝒯HE FERRIS WHEEL WHISKED VISITORS HIGH
ABOVE THE TRI-STATE FAIR SOMETIME IN THE
1910S. IN THE DISTANCE THE MIDWAY FREAK-
SHOW TENTS ADVERTISED SUCH ATTRACTIONS AS
"AMERICA'S LARGEST SISTERS" AND A TROUPE OF
THE "SMALLEST PERFORMING MIDGETS."

*P*eople lined up and paid 10 cents to go for a simulated ride "Over the Falls" in 1918. For those in doubt, the electric signs at the gate assured crowds that, "society attends" and urged them to "go see it everybody."

*T*he Pippin roller coaster, made completely of wood, gave young riders a thrill back in 1940.

Noah's Ark was a popular ride from 1922 until it was torn down in the early 1960s.

The Grand Carousel merry-go-round was built in 1909 in Chicago and has been at the fair since 1923.

The Tumble Bug rose and fell and twirled riders around as it ran along a network of tracks in 1954.

The Round-Up used centrifugal force to glue riders to its walls as they spun round and round in the early 1950s.

Visitors to the fair in 1971 could go for a wild ride on the Rampage double Ferris wheel.

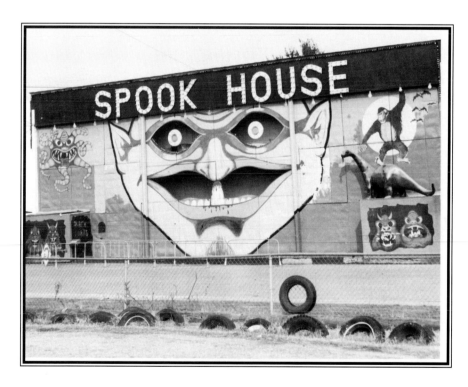

The Spook House as it looked in 1974. The graffiti that said "Death Awaits" was prophetic since the attraction was torn down soon after this to make way for Libertyland theme park.

*T*he amusement park as it looked at the 1954 Mid-South Fair. This site later became Libertyland theme park.

*T*he Old Mill boat ride was another long-lasting and popular attraction. Here is the ride in 1974 just before it was torn down to make way for Libertyland. Behind it is the Pippin; the roller coaster and the Grand Carousel were the only rides from the old amusement park that remained after Libertyland was built.

𝒫RONTO PUPS WERE A BIG ATTRAC-

TION FOR KIDS AS WELL AS ADULTS FOR

MANY YEARS AT THE FAIR, AND WERE AS

POPULAR IN THIS 1972 PHOTOGRAPH AS

THEY ARE TODAY.

A handful of cotton candy satisfied the sweet tooth of a seven-month-old girl as she spent the day with her parents at the 1974 fair.

*I*ce cream gave these sisters a reason to sit down and relax for a moment at the 1974 fair.

*T*ce cream also provided a nice break for these women at the 1972 fair.

*W*atching the taffy-pulling machine shape the sticky goo was fascinating to these teenagers at the fair in 1976.

*T*wo 15-year-olds paused for just a moment before devouring their warm, crisp elephant ears covered with powdered sugar, at the 1976 fair.

*P*ronto Pups are a must for all fair-goers at one time or another.

*C*orn-on-the-Cob was a father/son event for this duo at the 1975 fair.

THIS COWBOY FELL TO THE GROUND WHEN THE BRONCO BUCKED HIM JUST SECONDS AFTER LEAVING THE GATE AT THE RODEO IN 1958.

A rider takes a spill in a rodeo in the early 1950s.

Roquefort the bull, kicked up his heels at the fair rodeo in 1960. Other bulls at the fair that year were named by children and included Yogi Bear, Howdie Doodie and Elvis.

The World Championship Rodeo was held in the Arena Building in the 1950s and early 1960s.

This bucking bronco gave a rough ride. The competition was a part of the World Championship Rodeo at the fair in 1983. The rodeo had moved indoors to the coliseum by the mid-1960s.

Calf scrambles drew crowds to the rodeos in the 1980s.

CHAPTER
Seven

Elvis

*I*N THE MIDDLE IS LINDA THOMPSON, ELVIS' GIRL-
FRIEND FOR FIVE YEARS IN THE 1970S, AS SHE
COMPETES TO BECOME MISS MID-SOUTH IN 1968.
SHE WAS UNSUCCESSFUL THAT YEAR, BUT KEPT TRY-
ING AND WON IT ALL IN 1970.

*E*lvis had a penchant for the Fairgrounds, especially the Dodgem car rides and the Pippin roller coaster. He used to rent the fairgrounds amusement park at midnight so that he and his friends could ride the rides all night. In fact, just days before his death, he rented Libertyland and rode the Pippin for almost two hours.

But the amusement park was not the only attraction Elvis found at the Mid-South Fair. He also had a penchant for contest winners. Two of his girlfriends were former Miss Mid-South Fairs, and one was a former Mid-South Fair Talent Contest winner and a Miss Mid-South Fair runner-up.

He also made a surprise appearance at the 1956 fair, three weeks after his first appearance on the Ed Sullivan show, just when his popularity was beginning to skyrocket.

*N*ot only did Linda Thompson become the 1970 Miss Mid-South Fair and Elvis Presley's girlfriend, but she also got to pose holding the "moon rock" in 1970 which was one of the biggest attractions at that year's Mid-South Fair. The rock, which astronauts had brought back from man's first trip to the moon one year earlier, had to be escorted to and from the fairgrounds by police in an armored car.

Ginger Alden, Miss Mid-South Fair in 1976, goes for a ride on the refurbished Grand Carousel at Libertyland with her attendants. She was thought to be the tallest Fair queen ever. Alden was Elvis' girlfriend at the time of his death in 1977.

Here's another shot of Miss Mid-South Fair 1970, Linda Thompson, running through the fairgrounds, with the Shelby County Building in the background.

*A*nita Wood — 1954 Youth Talent Contest winner and former girlfriend of Elvis in the 1950s before Priscilla. In 1956 Wood was also a runner-up in the Fairest of the Fair competition. Elvis' manager, Colonel Parker, stopped them from marrying to preserve Elvis' bachelor image.

CHAPTER
Eight

Fairgrounds

This earliest picture available of the old
Montgomery Driving Park, which later
became the fairgrounds, was taken in 1895.
It shows the old race track's grandstand.

This was taken in 1895 as well, and shows the race track with what appears to be stables in the distance.

Another view of the grandstand taken in 1900.

THE GRANDSTAND AT MONTGOMERY DRIVING PARK CROWDED WITH PEOPLE IN 1907 DURING THE RACING SEASON AND ONE YEAR BEFORE THE FIRST TRI-STATE FAIR WAS HELD ON THESE GROUNDS.

This aerial view of the fairgrounds was taken sometime in the 1930s. It's facing south with the Woman's Building in the foreground in front of the Pippin. The first round structure is the Grand Carousel; the second round structure is the Casino Building. Just to the left of that is the old grandstand facing the track which by then had been reduced from a one-mile track to a half-mile track. East Parkway borders the western (left-hand) side of this picture.

This photo from the late forties or early fifties shows the race track after the old grandstand burned down and was made into what was called a speed bowl. This photo is taken facing north from Southern Avenue and shows how the fairgrounds looked before the Coliseum was built.

The north end of the fairgrounds in 1963, taken from East Parkway looking east. The Shelby County Building is in the upper right-hand corner of the shot with the livestock barns behind and beside it. This is before the Liberty Bowl Stadium was built.

*A view looking South of the fairgrounds in 1963.
The Coliseum is being built in the left-hand corner.*

*This 1970 photo shows the midway of the fair with both the stadium
and the coliseum in the background.*

BUILDINGS

EXPOSITION BUILDING.

AN EARLY DRAWING OF THE OLD EXPOSITION

BUILDING AT THE FAIRGROUNDS.

*F*air-goers crowd outside the entrance to the Tri-State Fair in 1912.

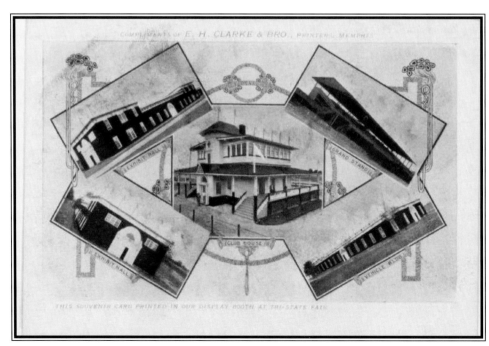

*T*his souvenir card was given out at the Tri-State Fair sometime in the 1910s. It shows the old Club House and the Grandstand, as well as two exhibit halls and the Vehicle Building.

*S*tables at the fairgrounds in 1916.

*T*he exterior of the Casino Building. Built in 1930, it had to be torn down in 1963 because it had fallen into disrepair. When the Casino first opened, admission was 40 cents.

A *view of the Shelby County Building in the 1920s during the fair.*

*T**he amusement park is crowded during an early 1930s fair. The round structure is the Grand Carousel and the Noah's Ark ride is in the left-hand bottom corner.*

*T**he Casino was readied for final demolition in August 1963.*

*T*he main gate of the fairgrounds on East Parkway welcomed fair visitors in 1958.

*T*he old glittering ball from the Casino dance floor was a lingering reminder of all the dancing and good times that had taken place there as the building was being torn down in 1963. The reflecting ball had originally cost $1,000.

A political rally in the 1950s where the Mid-South Coliseum now stands.

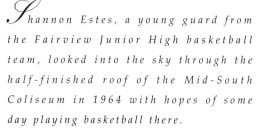

*S*hannon Estes, a young guard from the Fairview Junior High basketball team, looked into the sky through the half-finished roof of the Mid-South Coliseum in 1964 with hopes of some day playing basketball there.

*T*he new Libertyland theme park was home to "the world's longest love seat," as recorded by the Guinness Book of World Records in 1976. The bench is made from a 110-foot fir log from Oregon. It had been at the Fairgrounds since 1964 when it was presented to the Mid-South Fair by the Lumbermen's Club of Memphis.

*T*HIS REPLICA OF THE MID-SOUTH FAIR OFFICE BUILDING

WAS MADE OF GUMDROPS, PEANUT BRITTLE AND OTHER CANDY

IN 1971, AND WAS TEMPTING TO A FAIR EMPLOYEE WHO

WORKED AT THE FAIR'S FAMILY LIVING CENTER WHERE THE

SWEET BUILDING WAS ON DISPLAY.

Other Uses of the Fairgrounds

1910 AVIATION MEET

*I*N APRIL 1910, SEVERAL THOUSAND MEMPHIANS WERE INTRO-DUCED TO THE WORLD OF FLYING MACHINES, OR AIRPLANES, WHEN, JUST SEVEN YEARS AFTER THE WRIGHT BROTHERS MADE THEIR FAMOUS FIRST FLIGHT, THE CITY HOSTED ONE OF THE FIRST NATIONAL AVIATION MEETS IN THE COUNTRY.

At one point, fliers got their planes to circle over the racetrack at a then amazing speed of almost 50 miles per hour.

Curtiss with passenger,
J. C. Mars.

*A*ll eyes were on Memphis as the National Aviation Meet at the Tri-State Fairgrounds went from April 7 through April 10. The most famous pilot who attended was Glenn H. Curtiss. Just one year after the meet, Curtiss began manufacturing airplanes for the United States Navy. Thousands of his planes were used during World War I.

The "Miss Memphis" after pilot Glenn Curtiss crashed the plane on April 9, 1910.

*A*t the meet there were three crashes as winds and the frail bamboo and canvas structures of the machines combined to make flying difficult. Luckily, there were no major injuries. And at one point, fliers got their planes to circle over the racetrack at a then amazing speed of almost 50 miles per hour.

Willard as he took off from the track at the Tri-State Fairgrounds.

*A*nother pilot, Charles Willard, prepared to fly.

Willard in mid-air.

Charles Willard crashed into a fence at the Tri-State Fairgrounds. He begged photographers not to take pictures of the plane wreck, but to no avail. Here Willard's broken plane is removed from the field.

The ill-fated flight of pilot J. C. "Bud" Mars landed him on the car of Mrs. Ernest Ritter of Marked Tree, Ark. who was injured by the propeller. Mars walked away from the crash with only minor cuts and bruises.

This photo of J. C. Mars' plane wreckage made the front page of the Memphis News-Scimitar on April 11, 1910.

Flood Refugee Camps • 1912 & 1937

1912 - Camp Crump

THREE MAJOR FLOODS AFFLICTED THE MID-SOUTH IN THE EARLY 20TH CENTURY. THE FIRST WAS IN 1912, THE SECOND IN 1927, AND THE MOST DEVASTATING WAS IN 1937. ON FEBRUARY 1, 1937 THE MISSISSIPPI RIVER AT MEMPHIS WAS THREE AND A HALF MILES WIDE. EACH TIME, MEMPHIS' LOCATION ON THE CHICKASAW BLUFFS PUT MOST OF THE CITY ABOVE THE FLOOD PLAIN. CONSEQUENTLY, THE CITY THEN DEALT WITH ANOTHER KIND OF FLOOD, A FLOOD OF REFUGEES FROM LOW-LYING AREAS OF MISSISSIPPI, ARKANSAS, MISSOURI AND KENTUCKY LOOKING FOR HELP.

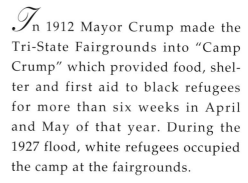

Black male refugees in 1912.

*I*n 1912 Mayor Crump made the Tri-State Fairgrounds into "Camp Crump" which provided food, shelter and first aid to black refugees for more than six weeks in April and May of that year. During the 1927 flood, white refugees occupied the camp at the fairgrounds.

By the time of the big flood of 1937, the Mid-South Fairgrounds were again used for white refugees from the area. More than 50,000 people poured in. They were housed in every imaginable place, including the Casino dance hall and several makeshift barracks built by the National Guard troops stationed at the fairgrounds. The refugees were tagged for identification and inoculated to prevent the spread of disease.

*R*efugees lined up for many services at Camp Crump, including food and first aid.

1937 Refugee Camp

The fairgrounds once again housed flood victims in 1937. This time, the refugees who stayed in the camp were white. The National Guard assisted in building temporary barracks to house the 1937 refugees.

*T*he "mess hall" at the refugee camp served flood victims meals of canned milk, bread and other food in 1937.

A first aid clinic was set up for refugees in 1937 at Fairview Junior High School at the Fairgrounds. It was administered by the National Guard.

The women and children stayed together in the barracks.

The chandelier lights and piano faded into the background as the Casino's wooden dance floor was crowded with beds of straw-stuffed mattresses to accommodate the women and children refugees in 1937. Decorations left over from Christmas dances hung overhead.

The males had separate sleeping quarters at the refugee camp in 1937. This is the same building that was used to showcase a four-man band at a radio station exhibit during the 1933 fair.

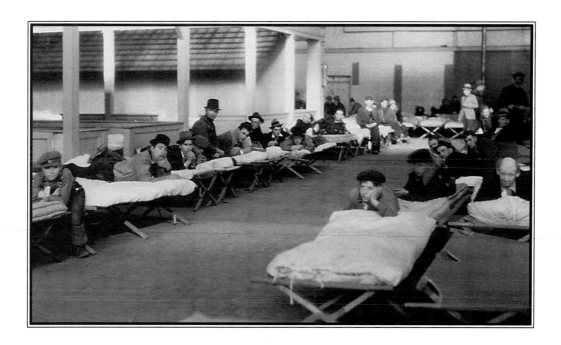

Mid-South Fair Presidents • General Managers

<table>
<tr><td colspan="2"><u>THE SHELBY COUNTY FAIR</u></td><td colspan="2"><u>THE MID-SOUTH FAIR</u></td></tr>
<tr><td colspan="2"><u>PRESIDENTS</u></td><td colspan="2"><u>PRESIDENTS</u></td></tr>
<tr><td>1856</td><td>Colonel John Pope</td><td></td><td></td></tr>
<tr><td>1857</td><td>Colonel John Pope</td><td>1929 - 1932</td><td>Lloyd T. Binford</td></tr>
<tr><td>1858</td><td>no available record</td><td>1933 - 1934</td><td>J.W. Shepherd</td></tr>
<tr><td>1859</td><td>no available record</td><td>1935 - 1943</td><td>Raymond Skinner</td></tr>
<tr><td>1860</td><td>no available record</td><td><u>WWII ERA</u></td><td><u>NO FAIRS 1942-1946</u></td></tr>
<tr><td></td><td></td><td>1944 - 1945</td><td>A. E. Harrold</td></tr>
<tr><td><u>CIVIL WAR ERA</u></td><td><u>NO FAIRS 1861-1867</u></td><td>1946</td><td>Martin Zook</td></tr>
<tr><td>1868</td><td>no available record</td><td>1947 - 1948</td><td>W.H. Dilatush</td></tr>
<tr><td>1869</td><td>Enoch Ensley</td><td>1949 - 1950</td><td>Perry Pipkin</td></tr>
<tr><td>1870</td><td>no available record</td><td>1951 - 1954</td><td>Lee T. Court</td></tr>
<tr><td>1871</td><td>Jacob Thompson</td><td>1955</td><td>Perry Pipkin</td></tr>
<tr><td>1872</td><td>Jacob Thompson</td><td>1956 - 1957</td><td>Wallace Witmer</td></tr>
<tr><td colspan="2"><u>THE TRI-STATE FAIR</u></td><td>1958 - 1959</td><td>Howard Tayloe</td></tr>
<tr><td>1908</td><td>Frederick Orgill</td><td>1960 - 1961</td><td>Boyd Arthur</td></tr>
<tr><td>1909</td><td>S.M. Neely</td><td>1962</td><td>Walter Dilatush</td></tr>
<tr><td>1910</td><td>S.M. Neely</td><td>1963</td><td>Weldon Burrow</td></tr>
<tr><td>1911 - 1917</td><td>A.L. Parker</td><td>1964 - 1968</td><td>Joe M. Pipkin</td></tr>
<tr><td>1918 - 1926</td><td>Charles A. Gerber</td><td>1969 - 1970</td><td>John Ellis</td></tr>
<tr><td>1927</td><td>O. P. Hurd</td><td>1971 - 1972</td><td>Lee Winchester</td></tr>
<tr><td>1928</td><td>Lloyd T. Binford</td><td>1973 - 1974</td><td>William H. Austin</td></tr>
<tr><td></td><td></td><td>1975 - 1976</td><td>Thomas F. O'Brien</td></tr>
<tr><td><u>MANAGERS</u></td><td></td><td>1977</td><td>Jack H. Morris, III</td></tr>
<tr><td>1908 - 1909</td><td>R.M. Williams</td><td>1978 - 1979</td><td>James W. Campbell, Jr.</td></tr>
<tr><td>1910 - 1938</td><td>Frank Fuller</td><td>1980 - 1981</td><td>William W. Farris</td></tr>
<tr><td>1939 - 1942</td><td>Henry Beaudoin</td><td>1982 - 1983</td><td>Olin F. Morris</td></tr>
<tr><td><u>WWII ERA</u></td><td><u>NO FAIRS 1942-1946</u></td><td>1984 - 1985</td><td>Daniel F. Wilkinson</td></tr>
<tr><td>1947</td><td>G.W. Wynne</td><td>1986 - 1987</td><td>Charles T. Pierotti</td></tr>
<tr><td>1948 - 1950</td><td>L. P. Herring, Jr.</td><td>1988 - 1989</td><td>Oscar Edmonds</td></tr>
<tr><td>1951 - 1954</td><td>Martin Zook</td><td>1990 - 1991</td><td>Debra Pace Branan</td></tr>
<tr><td>1955 - 1966</td><td>G.W. Wynne</td><td>1992 - 1993</td><td>Robert I. Bowers</td></tr>
<tr><td>1967 - 1977</td><td>T. Wilson Sparks</td><td>1994 - 1995</td><td>Robert O. Jamison</td></tr>
<tr><td>1978 - 1980</td><td>M. N. "Nat" Baxter</td><td>1996 - 1997</td><td>William E. Todd</td></tr>
<tr><td>1980 - 1981</td><td>Tom Batchelor</td><td></td><td></td></tr>
<tr><td>1982 - 1985</td><td>Robert Nichols</td><td></td><td></td></tr>
<tr><td>1985 - Present</td><td>Milton Rodgers</td><td></td><td></td></tr>
</table>

B I B L I O G R A P H Y

Memphis Magazine

The Commercial Appeal

The Memphis Press-Scimitar

Mid-South Magazine

The Daily Argus

The Evening Appeal

The Memphis Daily Appeal

The Memphis Daily Bulletin

Memphis Public Ledger

The Daily Avalanche

The World Book Encyclopedia

The Concise Columbia Encyclopedia

Encyclopaedia Britannica

Plunkett, Kitty, <u>A Pictorial History Memphis</u>, Donning Company Publishers, Norfolk, VA, 1976

Crawford, Charles, <u>Yesterday's Memphis</u>, E. A. Seemann Publishing, Inc., 1976

Harkins, John E., <u>Metropolis of the American Nile</u>, Guild Bindery Press,1991

Coppock, Paul, <u>Memphis Sketches</u>, Friends of Memphis and Shelby County Libraries, 1976

Memphis Symphony League, <u>Gracious Goodness - The Taste of Memphis</u>, 1989

Winfield, Loyce S., <u>1981 Mid-South Fair Official Guide</u>, 1981

Boom, Aaron M., "Early Fairs in Shelby County," <u>The West Tennessee Historical Society Papers</u>, 1956, No. X, p. 38

Shelby County Agricultural, Mechanical and Horticultural Society, <u>First Fair of the Society - Schedule of Premiums,</u> 1869

Shelby County Agricultural and Mechanical Society, <u>Third Annual Fair of the Society - Schedule of Premiums,</u> 1871

Memphis Commission Government, Aug. & Sept. 1913

Memphis Chamber of Commerce Journal, July, 1918

Fair committee minutes 1916-1923

Sigafroos, Robert, <u>Cotton Row to Beale Street</u>, pp. 118-119

Memphis Chamber of Commerce Journal, Sept., 1920

List of Premiums and Special Features of the Women's Department, Tri-State Fair, 1921

List of Premiums and Special Features of the Women's Department, Tri-State Fair, 1921

The Story of the Fair - A Synopsis of the 1924 Program and Other Interesting Information, Tri-State Fair, 1924

21st Annual Tri-State Fair Premium List, 1927

22nd Annual Tri-State Fair Premium List , 1928

Mid-South Fair Premium List, 1936

Mid-South Fair and Livestock Show - Premium List, 1947

Mid-South Fair and Livestock Show - Premium List, 1948

Mid-South Fair and Livestock Show - Premium List, 1950

Mid-South Fair and Livestock Show - Premium List, 1953

Mid-South Fair and Livestock Show - Premium List, 1954

Mid-South Fair and Livestock Show - Premium List, 1955

Mid-South Fair Centennial - Official Program, 1956

Hopkins, Jerry, Elvis: A Biography, 1971

The Daily Express - Lancashire, England 7/19/77, (Elvis) pp.16, 17

Mid-South Fair papers re: Centennial and Centennial Village

Mid-South Fair papers re: Talent winners

Mid-South Fair papers re: History of fair

Copy of telegram from Dwight D. Eisenhower 9/8/56

Mid-South Fair Poster - 1960

Mid-South Fair - Premium List, 1963

Youth Talent Winners List - 1960s (MSF offices)

Operating budget - 1962 (MSF offices)

Souvenir Program - 1971

Souvenir Program - 1972

Premium List - 1973

Fair Facts - 1974

Souvenir Program - 1975

Fair Program Brochure - 1978

Daily Program - 1979

The American Showman - November 1979

Mid-South Fair - Premium List - 1984

Fair Program Brochure - 1982

MSF Handbook - 1987

MSF Media Handbook and Directory - 1989

MSF Media Handbook and Directory - 1990

MSF Media Handbook and Directory - 1991

Roller Coaster! - Winter 1991

MSF Media Handbook and Directory - 1992

MSF-Premium Lists - Horticulture/Creative Arts - 1993